NOTES FROM A
Small Kitchen Island

Debora Robertson

Photography by Laura Edwards

MICHAEL
JOSEPH

For my mother, Wendy Robertson,
who encouraged me to cook and then to write it all down.

~

Contents

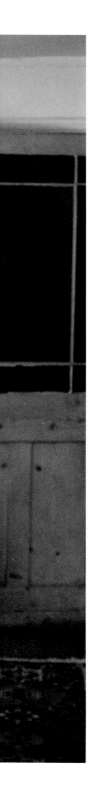

Introduction

Everything I know about life I learned in the kitchen.

~

I'VE BEEN TO A LOT OF PLACES. I've cooked a lot of things. But I am never more content than when I am in my London kitchen, wondering what we will have for dinner.

This is a book of essays with the recipes that made me, just as I made them. I describe how I learned to love cooking, from the least promising of starts. I come from a long line of working women who viewed the kitchen as hostile territory, but from my earliest days it was my favourite playground.

On these pages are stories of my favourite meals, foreign and domestic, from baking margarita pie one golden Texan summer and cooking dinners for diplomats in my tiny Moscow kitchen to the lazy feasts I make every summer in my favourite village in the Languedoc, and Turkish-ish weeknight dinners tumbled together with ingredients foraged (this is the only foraging I do, obviously; I don't have the shoes or the temperament for the other sort) from my local Turkish supermarket in Hackney, East London.

In this book I share my secrets for creating delicious meals every single day, without pretending to weave my own water or knit my own tahini. I describe some of the life- and dinner-saving lessons I've learned in all the kitchens I have cooked in, and share the daring tales of disaster too. Because there are always disasters – the inedible in chase of the unInstagrammable.

All the chapters are shot through with tales of my London life, because London is every place, a city where myriad cultures mix, where every ingredient is available, and every single one comes with a story, once upon a dinner time.

Chapter 1

Not like Mother used to make

ALMOST ALL THE GREAT COOKS I KNOW – and I know a lot of great cooks – have reams of family recipes to draw upon. You compliment them on the perfection of their pastry or the just-so seasoning of their noodles, and it's met with a shrug and, 'Oh, that's my mother's, my auntie's, my grandmother's recipe . . .' Their Instagram accounts and their book jackets feature pictures of them as children standing on chairs at the stove or at the kitchen counter, stirring something, flour on their aprons, chocolate around their mouths. Adorable.

Meet my family.

My grandmother's proudest – and only – kitchen boast was that during the Blitz in Coventry, my grandfather made her a kitchen table from reinforced steel so they could hide under it if getting themselves and four small children into an air-raid shelter in the middle of the night proved too challenging. This is literally my only family-related food story. Where others have Lancashire hot pot and fondant fancies, my kitchen heritage centres on defying the Luftwaffe.

My mother, born in 1941, grew up without any great interest in food, as what there was of it was not very interesting. As she explains, if she'd loved or cared about dinner, she would have lived in a landscape of persistent, gnawing disappointment. To this day, she could cheerfully live on smoked salmon sandwiches.

When my grandfather died, my grandmother and her children – my mother, her sister, Susan, and brothers, Tom and Ian – moved from Coventry back to County Durham to be closer to her family. She got a job in a factory and later became a nurse in a psychiatric hospital. My first memory is being held in my grandmother's arms next to a stall at the hospital's summer fête. She often used to take me to see 'her ladies'. Many of them had spent years in the hospital, and I was the first baby they'd seen since they had had or had lost babies of their own, decades before. Years later, they still asked about the baby. I was almost an adult by then, I think. Time stood still.

Anyway, my mother was the first in her family to go to college. When my brother, Grahame, and I were small, she was teaching, taking another degree in the evenings, going to talks on feminism where I sat on the floor with paper and crayons. Grahame wasn't welcome at the meetings despite being all of four or five years old because: patriarchy. At weekends, my mother wrote children's novels and wrangled our large Victorian house into submission, one eye on Jocasta Innes's *The Pauper's Homemaking Book*, one eye on the clock.

There wasn't much time for carefully tended stews, despite JI's *Pauper's Cookbook* also sitting on the shelves, somewhere. We had a lot of things on toast – scrambled eggs, beans, something called, helpfully, toast toppers, which was essentially a thickened cream of mushroom soup. Even though this was the era of potato waffles and crispy pancakes, those were seen as too expensive, not quite the thing. I do, however, have an abiding love for fish fingers, which were somehow allowed.

I can cook because my mother can't. I mean, really can't. To her the kitchen is hostile territory where pans commit scorching hara-kiri and ovens

spontaneously combust. She would have rather been anywhere else. Which, conveniently, allowed the kitchen to become my happily anarchic playground.

In friends' houses, the kitchens were most definitely their mothers' territory. We might be allowed to distract ourselves after school by making a Victoria sponge from a Green's cake mix, but that was quite enough self-expression, thank you.

At home, I could make anything. With the *Hamlyn All Colour Cookbook* by my side, and Marguerite Patten as my pretend mother, I worked my way through chicken Mornay (sprinkled with cheese and crushed cornflakes), crunchy-topped fish bake (plaice cooked in tinned cream of mushroom soup, finished with a handful of crisps and anchovies), sherried kidneys, Bakewell tart, devil's food cake with marshmallow frosting, curried egg salad . . . All the 1970s greats.

My parents entertained a lot. Women in flowing dresses sat around while exuberantly sideburned men played folk songs on the guitar. Or Glen Campbell ('and I need you more than want you, and I want you for all tiiiimmmme') played on the stereo, though that was more something my mother listened to in the afternoon, with our neighbour Bernice, over sticky glasses of sherry or Cinzano.

For these parties, my mother might make coq au vin or spaghetti Bolognese, with more efficiency than passion. Or she might not. In that case, I would be there passing around canapés I'd concocted like a tiny Margot Leadbetter. I remember a tuna fish pâté which was essentially tinned tuna beaten with softened butter and a squeeze of juice from a squeezy plastic lemon, dash of pepper from a tub, spread on to Jacob's crackers, mushroom vol-au-vents (tinned condensed mushroom soup was in high rotation in the 70s kitchen), cheese balls rolled in toasted nuts, all kinds of things on cocktail sticks. And an elaborate apple charlotte made using every implement in the kitchen. I just made what I wanted. Still do. I am just a little better at putting things together and I set my own bedtime.

Auntie Louie's corned beef and potato pie

SERVES ~ **6–8**

My grandmother Barbara had four sisters, Lily, Dolly, Louie and Alice. They all had good hands and put them to use: knitting, sewing, crocheting, decorating – the Welsh chapel belief that the devil made work for idle hands ran deep with them. (And down the generations. I still find it hard to sit and do nothing.) At the end of their lives, my grandmother, Dolly and Louie all lived in the same street, so I was often in and out of all their houses. Auntie Louie was a wonderful baker and there was always something delicious in a tin in her house – a scone, a rock bun, a fairy cake. This corned beef pie is the taste of my childhood, give or take a few embellishments (it's a long way from flaky sea salt I was raised), served with butterhead lettuce, a slice of tomato and cucumber, and a dollop of salad cream.

FOR THE PASTRY

380g plain flour

¾ teaspoon salt

¼ teaspoon freshly ground black pepper

110g unsalted butter, very cold, cut into small cubes

100g lard, very cold, cut into small cubes

120–140ml iced water

FOR THE PIE FILLING

30g unsalted butter

2 medium-sized onions, about 340g total weight, halved and thinly sliced

240g waxy potatoes, peeled and cut into 1.5cm cubes

180ml beef stock (make it from a stock cube if you want)

1 tablespoon Worcestershire sauce

1 tablespoon fresh thyme leaves, roughly chopped

salt and freshly ground black pepper

100g frozen peas (garden peas ideally, but petits pois are also fine, we're not going to fall out over peas)

1 x 340g tin of corned beef, cut into 2cm cubes

3 tablespoons chopped fresh parsley leaves

FOR THE TOP

3 tablespoons cream, double or single, or whole milk, flaky sea salt and freshly ground black pepper

First, make the pastry. Tip the flour into a bowl and whisk in the salt and pepper. Add the butter and lard and rub it together with your fingertips until it mostly resembles coarse crumbs – leave some pea-sized lumps in the mixture, which will help make the pastry flaky and light. Trickle on 120ml of water and cut it in with

a dinner knife to form a dough – you might need slightly more water, but add just enough to bring it together. Turn it out on to a sheet of cling film and pat it together into a round. Wrap it up and refrigerate it for at least an hour. You can make the pastry up to this point a day ahead.

In a large frying pan, warm the butter over a medium–low heat and fry the onions and potatoes for about 10 minutes, stirring from time to time. Add the stock, Worcestershire sauce, thyme, ½ teaspoon of pepper and a good pinch of salt and simmer gently for 15 minutes or so, covered, until the potatoes are completely cooked through. Take the lid off and simmer until the stock is reduced – you don't want it to be at all soggy. Remove from the heat and stir in the peas. Taste, add more salt and pepper if it needs it, and leave to cool. Fold in the corned beef and parsley.

Preheat the oven to 190°C/170°C fan/gas 5.

Break off just over half the pastry and roll it out on a lightly floured surface with a floured rolling pin (or see TIP). Line a pie plate or tin; the one I use is 24cm diameter by 4cm deep. Trim off excess pastry and brush the edges lightly with milk or cream. Spoon in the corned beef filling, then roll out the remaining pastry, cover the pie, trim the excess pastry and then pinch together the edges – you can either crimp them fancily or just press them together with the back of a fork. Cut a hole in the top of the pastry for the steam to escape and, if you like, decorate the top with the trimmed-off pastry cut into leaves, circles, squiggles . . .

Brush the top with milk or cream, sprinkle on some flaky sea salt and pepper, place the plate on a baking tray to collect any drips, and bake until well browned, about 45–50 minutes.

TIP

If you are at all nervous about working with pastry, rolling it out between two sheets of baking parchment or cling film lightly dusted with flour, then chilling it in the fridge for 15 minutes before handling it, will help.

~

Leek and ham hock steamed pudding

SERVES ~ 4–6

Back when schools still had proper kitchens, my favourite lunch at Bessemer Park Infant School was steamed leek pudding, which the doughy-armed cook made like a savoury roly-poly. I have been a fan of steamed puddings ever since, savoury and sweet, rolled and pudding basin'd. This one remains an enormous favourite. Adding mustard powder and cheese to the suet crust is really a gift you will want to keep giving yourself. I serve it very simply, with just some carrots and green beans in the manner of northern school dinners of yore. Sometimes I make it filled solely with leeks and serve it alongside a roast – it's wonderful for soaking up a rich meat gravy. Weirdly for such a comfortingly old-fashioned dish, when I posted a picture of this pudding on my Twitter and Instagram accounts, I got thousands of likes and responses, so many you would think I had just invented avocado toast.

FOR THE PASTRY
280g self-raising flour, plus a little more for rolling out

140g shredded suet (beef or vegetable)

40g finely grated Cheddar cheese

1 teaspoon English mustard powder

1 teaspoon salt

½ teaspoon freshly ground black pepper

about 160ml chilled whole milk

FOR THE FILLING
50g unsalted butter, plus more for greasing the bowl and baking parchment

4 medium leeks, about 450g, white and pale green part only, finely sliced and washed well

salt and freshly ground black pepper

150g cooked, roughly shredded ham hock

70ml double cream

1 teaspoon Dijon mustard

1 teaspoon fresh thyme leaves

Mix the flour and suet with the cheese, mustard, salt and pepper. Combine with enough milk to make a stiffish dough – you may need a little more or less than 160ml, depending on the flour, the day, the humidity in your kitchen – add about 140ml, then add in splashes until you get the right consistency. Form into a disc and chill the dough in the fridge while you prepare the rest.

Melt the butter in a frying pan over a medium–low heat and gently sauté the leeks with a good pinch of salt and pepper until soft, about 15 minutes. Move the pan from the heat and stir in the ham hock, cream, mustard and thyme. Cool. On a lightly floured surface, roll out the dough into a large circle, approximately 30cm in diameter. Cut a quarter out of the circle. Generously butter a 1.2 litre pudding basin and line it by dropping the larger piece of pastry into it, brushing the cut edges lightly with water, then drawing them together to make a firm join. Fill with the leek and ham hock mixture. Roll out the remaining quarter of pastry into a circle. Brush the pastry rim lightly with water and lay the circle on top. Pinch together the edges of the pastry lid and casing to seal. Put a double layer of buttered, pleated baking parchment over the top and tie in place with string, or you can just cover tightly with buttered foil if you can't be bothered with the faff. I am giving you both the Gold Standard and the That'll Do methods here.

Put a large pan of water on to boil (fill the pan with enough water to come a little more than halfway up the side of the basin), and place an upturned tart tin or saucer in the bottom to act as a trivet. Lower the pudding on to the makeshift trivet, put the lid on the pan and leave to simmer for 2 hours. Check from time to time and if the water gets low, top it up with boiling water from the kettle.

Remove the bowl carefully from the pan, take off the baking parchment, run a knife around the edge of the pudding, invert it on to a plate and serve hot.

VARIATION

Instead of the ham hock, use 6 slices of unsmoked back bacon, cut into 2cm pieces. Sauté the bacon in the melted butter until just becoming crisp, then remove with a slotted spoon and set aside. Sauté the leeks in the butter and bacon fat, as above, before combining the leeks and bacon with the cream.

~

Roast lamb with Durham salad

SERVES ~ 6

My slow-roast lamb is luscious and garlicky, which would probably have offended my northern antecedents, who greeted the arrival of garlic in the trattorias and brasseries of County Durham circa 1970 with no small amount of suspicion, bordering on disdain. My mother, being a free spirit and one of the first people in the county to wear cork wedges, suede trouser suits and, famously, a crocheted bikini made by my Auntie Dolly, was an early adopter and always loved, and still loves, garlic, so this is for her.

Durham salad, always present on the Sunday lunch table of my childhood, is northern salsa verde. Sometimes it's made with the vinegar from a jar of pickled onions, sometimes just plain old malt vinegar. Today, embracing my fancy London ways, I make it with white wine vinegar. Even with this concession, you certainly know it's there. I like the simple sweetness of buttered carrots with this. They are enough. If there is any Durham salad left over, it is lovely tossed with boiled new potatoes.

2kg leg or shoulder of lamb

1.3kg potatoes (Desirée or Maris Piper work well), peeled and thinly sliced, about 3mm thick (see TIP, page 18)

3 medium onions, about 500g, halved and thinly sliced

1 leek, white and pale green part only, about 100g, thinly sliced

4 bay leaves

4 sprigs of fresh thyme

salt and freshly ground black pepper

800ml lamb or chicken stock

5–6 cloves of garlic, halved, any green germ removed

70g butter, melted

1 tablespoon Worcestershire sauce

1 teaspoon Marmite

FOR THE DURHAM SALAD

1 bunch of fresh mint, about 25g, stalks removed and discarded

4–5 soft lettuce leaves, about 25g

2 teaspoons caster sugar

1 spring onion, trimmed and very finely chopped

90ml white wine vinegar

Remove the lamb from the fridge at least an hour before you want to cook it, so it can come to room temperature. Preheat the oven to 160°C/140°C fan/gas 3.

Line the bottom of a large, heavy roasting tin or earthenware dish – I use one that is 30 × 24 × 10cm – with half the potatoes. Scatter over the onions, leeks and herbs and season with salt and pepper. Add the remaining potatoes and pour over the stock.

Pierce the lamb in 10 to 12 places with a small, sharp knife. Insert the garlic into the cuts. Put the lamb on top of the potatoes, skin side up. Whisk together the butter, Worcestershire sauce and Marmite and brush it all over the lamb, letting any excess trickle on to the potatoes. Grind on a generous amount of pepper.

Cover the tin or dish tightly with foil and place in the oven for 3 hours. Remove the foil (save it for when you are resting the meat) and roast for a further 1½–2 hours, until the meat is very tender and the potatoes have absorbed most of the liquid. Place the lamb on a warm serving platter and cover loosely with foil while you finish the potatoes. Turn the oven up to 190°C/170°C fan/gas 5 and return the vegetables to the oven to crisp up on top for 20–30 minutes.

While the meat is resting and the vegetables are crisping up, make the Durham salad. Place the mint and lettuce on a chopping board and sprinkle over the sugar. Shred them very finely with a sharp knife, then tip into a bowl with the spring onion. Stir in the vinegar and leave to macerate for 15 minutes before serving with the roast lamb and the potatoes, perhaps with some simply boiled, buttered carrots on the side.

TIP

I have sliced off the tips of my fingers with a mandolin more times than I care to remember, so I am very wary of them, even though I now have a chain mail glove which is supposed to make them safer. I still don't trust the cursèd implements, so I prefer to use a sharp knife and take my time. But you may well be braver than me. Slice on, you crazy diamond.

~

Stoke Newington,
mon amour

MORE THAN TWENTY YEARS AGO, WHEN SÉAN AND I WERE NEWLY
MARRIED and looking for our first flat in Stoke Newington, we went to
see a place off the High Street, our hands clutching crudely printed estate
agents' details and our hearts full of hope. Directly in front of the flat was a
burned-out car and a sagging, stained sofa. As we walked towards the front
door, a rat jumped out of a damp cushion and skittered across the path in
front of us. There is only so much a Philippe Starke citrus juicer and an
orange statement wall can do, and it wasn't enough to win us over to this
fixer-upper. We consoled ourselves with cappuccinos and damp quiche
in The Cooler, a café on Church Street whose name was possibly derived
from the chilly welcome. No one knows. It closed soon afterwards. Word
got around that the owners had done a flit and the staff were selling off
bags of pasta and organic granola at bargain prices to make up their wages.
Wholesome Hackneyites gathered in the shop, with the slight sense of
urgency and shame that during the war the borough's residents might have
displayed when furtively buying nylons and fags from black-market spivs.

Eventually we found a place, a flat in a Victorian house on Brooke Road with a large, bright, bay-windowed sitting room, a fireplace, wooden floors, essentially the late-90s dream. Downstairs there was a small, square kitchen big enough to hold a small, square table and four tatty chairs. It had a door which opened on to the garden. This was just as well, because I bought a huge, American fridge when such things were still quite new. It was too big to come in the front door, so it had to be heaved through the bay window at the front, carried across the sitting room, lowered two floors out of the dining-room window, hauled across the garden and then finally into the kitchen through the garden door. I guess you had to really want a chilled water dispenser, and I guess I really did.

We painted the cabinets emerald green, installed a thick wooden counter and a white butler's sink, and tucked a shiny cream stove with six burners into the gap where the old fireplace once was. Outside the kitchen door I planted pots with thyme, tarragon, rosemary, mint, bay and parsley, though I soon realized I could never grow as much parsley as I used and that I could buy huge bunches of it for less than a quid at one of the many Turkish supermarkets dotted along the High Street. Ditto coriander and dill.

During the day, I pitched magazine articles, balancing my enthusiasm with a gnawing fear of rejection. In the evening, I cooked and cooked. We'd only known each other for six weeks when we got engaged. It was all brand new, gentle, exciting. We ate dinner at the little kitchen table, getting to know one another and working out what our life together would look like over roast chickens and bowls of garlicky pasta. We acquired two kittens, and when we managed to keep them alive, made an attempt at creating human babies, which was a less successful experiment.

We filled our lives with friends, old ones and new ones. I developed then a habit which has never left me of celebrating life at every possible opportunity. Burns Night, Pancake Day, St Patrick's Day, Easter,

Midsummer's Day, Bastille Day, Christmas, New Year's Eve, my calendar was filled with food, menus, friends. We had lots of parties, where we plated up on the garden table because we had so little counter space and then raced the food up the short flight of stairs into the dining room before it was too cold and we were too hot. I tried not to think of how sniffily I had rejected my mother-in-law's offer of a hostess trolley for a wedding present.

I went shopping at Ridley Road market, scooping £1 bowls of fruit and veg into my shopping trolley, and at Egg Stores, the kosher grocers on Stamford Hill, for schmaltz herring and tubs of chrain, the tear-inducing condiment of grated horseradish and beetroot. I went to Gallo Nero on the High Street for thin slices of finocchiona, fat *salsiccia fresca*, rough wedges of Parmesan, pots of their pesto and bottles of olive oil from their farm in Tuscany. Sometimes, I bought a bowl or two of tiramisù made by the owner Michele's mum. From the Mediterranean Supermarket, I picked up tubs of feta in brine, olives and fat bunches of herbs.

Over the past twenty years a lot has changed in Stoke Newington, and also not much. It's easy to think that today Stokey's more Boden than bohemian, but it's still grimy and noisy and you never quite know what you'll see when you leave the house. It's a little more polished, a little less weird. Today's house-hunting couples work in the City, or law, or are something in tech at Old Street, London's Silicon Roundabout – doing jobs that didn't exist twenty years ago. The jazz club is now a Nando's (for a while, a noisy group of chicken-resisters took up a position on the roof, hanging from it a large red and black banner: 'Existence is Resistance'). Whincops wood merchants is a Wholefoods, the Mediterranean Supermarket an organic supermarket, General Woodwork a Sainsbury's. Junk & Disorderly, where I bought fine linen sheets, ex-hotel stock, not quite perfect but perfect enough for me, is now a smart gift shop selling £30 notebooks and £50 candles.

Nothing stays the same. We moved from that pretty flat with its emerald green kitchen into a house just round the corner, where we built a big kitchen on the back with bi-fold doors and a glass ceiling, in line with the prevailing East London aesthetic. We installed a slab of Carrara marble – the kitchen island which became a column and then this book – I bought from an Irish builder called Jimmy who specialized in restoring altars for the Catholic Church. It is my own altar of sorts. We live our lives around it, measuring the passing of months and years in peaceful dinners together and loud parties, with crowds of friends gathered both around the island and into our lives. Its honed, bull-nose edges are now shiny from people sitting and leaning up against them, its once-perfect finish etched with the ghostly marks of lemon wedges, splashes of wine, the patina of a life lived.

Fox Reformed smoked haddock in tarragon cream

SERVES ~ 2

In the mid-90s when I was newly engaged to Séan, he took me to this little restaurant in Stoke Newington for dinner. The exterior of the Fox Reformed was painted a dark, wine red, and the windows were filled with a jumble of corks from bottles past. Inside, the room was long and narrow, with a bar on the left where regulars chatted with the owners, Robbie and Carole. A fire crackled in the grate, and at two or three tables people were playing backgammon. The menu never really changed – salads, gratins, daubes, steaks. That first evening, and almost every time I went after that, I had the smoked haddock in tarragon cream to start. I have dressed it up here with an egg and some cheese, so you could serve it as a brunch or lunch dish on its own if you wanted, but I have included the very simple and very good original as an alternative, below.

When Carole Richards gave me the recipe just before she died, she included the instruction, 'Serve with agreeable bread to mop up.' And I always do.

a little soft butter for the ramekins

170ml double cream

2 tablespoons roughly chopped fresh tarragon leaves

1 teaspoon Dijon mustard

a few grinds of black pepper

170g smoked haddock, uncooked, skinned and cut into roughly 2cm chunks

2 eggs

20g Gruyère cheese, finely grated

TO SERVE
agreeable bread, or toast

Preheat the oven to 220°C/200°C fan/gas 7. Lightly butter two 250ml ovenproof dishes or generous ramekins.

Pour the cream into a pan with the tarragon and bring to a simmer. Reduce until thickened slightly, then remove from the heat and stir in the mustard and black pepper.

Heap half the haddock into one of the dishes, making a small well in the centre of it. Break one of the eggs into the middle – you want it to nestle in the centre of the fish. Pour half the tarragon cream over the top and sprinkle on half the cheese. Repeat with the second ramekin. Cover each dish tightly with foil and place them on a baking sheet. Heat up the grill. Place the dishes in the oven and bake for 5 minutes. Remove the foil and put the dishes under a hot grill for a

minute or so, until bubbling and golden. Serve immediately, with agreeable bread or toast, to dip into the still-soft egg yolks.

ORIGINAL VERSION

To make the simpler, original version, make the tarragon cream, stir in the haddock and gently warm it – you don't want to cook it all the way through, as it will be tough. Divide the mixture between two ovenproof dishes and place under a fiercely hot grill, or blast with a chef's blowtorch, until nicely browned.

~

Farmers' market green salad

SERVES ~ 4

In 2003, Growing Communities set up a farmers' market in Stoke Newington. It was, possibly still is, the country's first wholly organic and biodynamic market. Back then, we barely knew what biodynamic meant but we knew we liked it, and trotting around the stalls in the courtyard of the Old Fire Station made us feel like extras in some sort of Nancy Meyers movie. We queued in the cold for goat's milk ice cream, which we pretended was delicious, we bought thick yoghurt in earthenware bowls, and chatted to a man with a wicker backpack who, when asked, said he had woven it himself. It was the most Stoke Newington of experiences. The market has grown since then and moved locations twice, but on Saturday afternoons I still enjoy wandering about the car park of St Paul's Church, picking out the makings of an organic, biodynamic lunch, then placing them in my own wicker basket, which I did not weave myself.

I love a leafy salad full of squeaky-fresh lettuce. At the market, Wild Country Organics has wonderful leaves every week, a pick-and-mix of mizuna, rocket, lamb's lettuce, purslane, shiso . . . in short, the sort of leaves that would put Mr McGregor's garden to shame with their exuberant freshness.

While I love all manner of salads, a simple green salad with great leaves, good oil, a splash of something acidic, a sprinkle of salt, is hard to beat. It is so much more than the sum of its parts. Add toasted nuts, shavings of cheese, some herbs if you wish, but it is so good just as it is. As Coco Chanel said, elegance is refusal.

Chapter 2 ~ Stoke Newington, *mon amour*

*1-ish tablespoon extra virgin olive oil,
the best you have*

*a couple of handfuls of leaves in a
high state of vitality, washed and
dried as described below*

*a squeeze of lemon juice or
a trickle of fine vinegar*

a pinch of flaky sea salt

Put the oil in the bottom of your salad bowl, then add the perfectly washed and dried leaves. You need far less oil than you think. Now, use your scrupulously clean and beautiful hands to gently toss the leaves so they are just glimmering with a slick of oil. Your hands are by far the best and gentlest salad spoons in existence. Next, squeeze on a little lemon or trickle the barest amount of vinegar over the top – coating with oil first stops the acidic element from burning the leaves and ensures it sits right on top, ready to leap on to your tongue. Sprinkle on a little salt and serve immediately.

If you are feeding a crowd and want to get ahead a little, pour the oil into the bottom of the bowl, put the leaves on top, and toss it all together just before you are ready to serve it.

TIP **HOW TO WASH SALAD**

I wash everything, even those bags of salad that proclaim there is no need to wash them. Equally important, and sometimes overlooked, is drying. Drying is vital. Your delicious dressing will slither off damp leaves, which is just too sad to contemplate.

Fill the sink or a large bowl with cold water. (I know this seems obvious, but I once watched an episode of *Real Housewives of Beverly Hills* where one of the women, on being instructed to wash a chicken, got out the washing-up liquid, so you never know. Oh, and also, never wash chicken.) Cut off the root of the lettuce and tear the leaves into bite-size pieces. Leave them in the sink for up to 15 minutes, then gently lift them into a colander or into the basket of a salad spinner, leaving the dirt behind. Rinse them again under running water. Next, if you have a salad spinner, whiz them around to remove excess moisture – don't overcrowd the leaves, and do it in several goes if you have to. If you don't have a salad spinner, gather them gently into a clean tea towel, go outside and spin them around with windmill arms, a human salad spinner in action. Next, lay them out on kitchen paper and gently roll them up, to absorb any excess moisture. If you want to prepare your salad ahead, put the lettuce-paper roll into a ziplock bag in the fridge, where they will remain perky for several days.

~

Stokey Lit Fest chilli for thirty or forty or so

SERVES ~ 30 or 40, depending on whatever else you are serving with it

Many of us, at some point or another, will need a recipe to feed a massive crowd and this is mine. Every June, Stoke Newington has its literary festival, which sprawls its way along Church Street and into the High Street, leaving scarcely a church hall, meeting room, gallery or pub undisturbed for one precious weekend of books and high jinks. Pink bunting festoons railings and pink-T-shirted volunteers are dotted around the streets, helping visitors with directions and the finer points of schedule management. On the last night, all of us who have been involved throughout the year with the planning and, in that one, bleary, magnificent weekend, with the execution, pile into the town hall in a state of happy hysteria to drink drinks and swap stories. Then we go over the road to Ryan's Bar because no one wants to go home. With this in mind, and with memories of trawling chip shops and kebab shops for sustenance in previous years, in 2019 I decided to make dinner for anyone who wanted it and this chilli was that. I led the pub-late crowd along the streets of Stoke Newington like a cumin-scented Pied Piper, and a couple of dozen of us ate bowls of chilli, drank more, and danced around the kitchen island. Sweet liaisons were made and a poet who shall remain nameless* was rebuffed and kicked the bin down the path on the way out. All in all, a perfect evening.

* I'm not being discreet – I'd tell you if I could – but I just can't remember who he was.

10 dried ancho chillies, for fruity sweetness

3–6 dried habanero chillies, for heat – you know how hot you like it

30g cumin seeds, about 5 tablespoons

10g coriander seeds, about 2 tablespoons

about 100ml vegetable oil

1kg smoked streaky bacon, cut into 1cm pieces

5kg chuck steak (stewing steak), cut into 2cm cubes

8–9 medium onions, about 1.5kg, diced

4 bay leaves

6 sticks of celery, about 350g, trimmed, any tough threads removed with a sharp vegetable peeler, and diced – save any leaves if you have them, to add at the end

20 cloves of garlic, halved, green germ removed, grated or pounded in a pestle and mortar, or whizzed in a small food processor into a smooth paste

170g concentrated tomato purée

2.5 litres beef stock

4 x 400g tins of plum tomatoes

680ml jar of passata

4 tablespoons red wine vinegar

$\longrightarrow$

3 tablespoons dried oregano

1 tablespoon cayenne pepper

1 teaspoon ground allspice

3 tablespoons freshly ground black pepper

2 tablespoons salt

6–12 jalapeño chillies, depending on their size and your taste, finely chopped, seeds and all – you could add 6, then keep adding a few more until you get the balance you like

100g dark chocolate, at least 70 per cent cocoa, but really the darker the better

juice of 4 limes (see **TIP**, page 212)

TO SERVE

any combination of grated Cheddar cheese, sour cream, sliced spring onions, chopped fresh coriander, quartered lime wedges, rice

Snip the stems from the chillies with scissors and tip out the seeds. In a small frying pan over a high heat, toast them on both sides for about 15 seconds until they puff up and soften, then add just enough water to cover. Remove from the heat and leave to soak for about 30 minutes. Drain the chillies, reserving a little of the water, then blend them in a mini chopper, with a stick blender or in a pestle and mortar with just enough of the soaking water to make a paste.

In another small pan, over a medium–high heat, toast the cumin and coriander seeds for about 30 seconds to a minute, until gently fragrant. Tip them on to a plate to cool, then pound them in a pestle and mortar or whiz them in a mini chopper or spice mill into a powder.

In a very large stockpot or casserole, warm the oil over a medium–high heat and fry the bacon until crisp. Remove it from the pan with a slotted spoon and put it on to a large platter while you begin to brown the meat (see TIP, page 228), which you will need to do in batches. As the meat browns, put it on to the platter with the bacon – you may need two platters, there's a lot of meat.

When you've browned all the meat, turn the heat down as low as you can, add the onions with a good pinch of salt and the bay leaves, fry gently, stirring frequently, until they're softened, about 20–30 minutes, then add the celery and sauté for another 5 minutes. Add the garlic, ground cumin and coriander and fry gently for a couple more minutes. Spoon in the tomato purée and chilli paste, stir for a minute, then add the stock, tinned tomatoes, passata, vinegar, oregano, cayenne pepper and allspice, and stir again. Simmer gently for 15 minutes, then return the bacon and beef to the pan, along with any juices which have accumulated on the plate/s, and the salt and pepper.

Bring to a simmer and cook, uncovered, very gently – the barest of blips breaking the surface – for 4 hours, until it is thick, rich and dark, and the meat is very tender. Check it every 30 minutes or so, give it a stir, and add some water if it looks dry. After the first couple of hours, check for seasoning too and add more salt and pepper if you think it needs it.

When the meat is very tender, add the jalapeño peppers, any reserved, chopped celery leaves if you have them, and the chocolate and cook for a further 10 minutes or so. Just before serving (with any of the suggested accompaniments you like), stir in the lime juice and taste again to adjust the seasoning one last time.

If you miraculously have any leftovers, it's even better the next day.

TIP

I use a massive 24-litre pot for this, bought fairly inexpensively in Dalston's Ridley Road market. It is aluminium and quite heavy, which is what you want as a thin pan is no good for slow cooking – you run the risk that the food on the bottom of the pan will scorch and stick. I use it quite a lot, not just for huge soups, stews and chillis, but also for making large batches of stock using several chickens. If you have room to store it, I think it is a good investment.

You can double this recipe quite easily, and if your crowd isn't as large as you anticipated, it freezes brilliantly.

~

Clissold Park Christmas crinkle cookies

MAKES ~ **36 cookies**

I've been to grander parties. This is a long way from silver trays of canapés in elegant hotels, or premier cru in posh houses fragrant with feu du bois Diptyque candles and money. But this is the party I look forward to as soon as I flip the calendar over to December. Every Christmas, those of us who walk our dogs in Clissold Park assemble in the breath-misting morning chill to swap stories, drink, eat. A picnic table quickly disappears beneath foil-wrapped and plastic-boxed Christmas treats, thermoses of coffee, paper napkins and plastic cups. Mulled wine, spiked coffee, sausage rolls, mince pies, large tins of Quality Street form a festive breakfast. I always take some biscuits for the dogs (see pages 159, 160) and these cookies, which I adapted years ago from an old Martha Stewart recipe. And I always leave the park wishing there were more parties to which it was acceptable to wear your gardening shoes.

120g dark chocolate, about 70 per cent, broken into small pieces

180g plain flour

50g cocoa powder

2 teaspoons baking powder

½ teaspoon salt

100g unsalted butter, room temperature

200g light muscovado sugar

2 eggs, lightly beaten

2 teaspoons vanilla extract

1 tablespoon Kahlua (optional)

80ml whole milk

caster sugar and sieved icing sugar, for rolling

Place the chocolate in a heatproof bowl over a pan of barely simmering water (the water should not touch the bottom of the bowl). Melt, stirring from time to time. Cool.

Whisk together the flour, cocoa powder, baking powder and salt in a bowl.

In a stand mixer or with a hand mixer, beat the butter until smooth, then add the sugar and beat until very light and fluffy – you will think there isn't enough butter, but keep going, it'll be fine. Add the eggs about a tablespoon at a time, beating until well combined after each addition. Beat in the vanilla and Kahlua if using, then the cooled chocolate.

With the beater/s on a low speed, add a third of the flour mixture, then half the milk, and repeat, ending with the last third of the flour. Mix until just combined. Be careful not to overmix or the cookies will be tough – the dough should be soft and cakey, rather mousse-y. Divide the dough into 2 flattish discs of about 400g each, wrap in cling film and refrigerate for at least 4 hours or overnight. You can make them a couple of days ahead to this point.

Preheat the oven to 180°C/160°C fan/gas 4. Line two baking sheets with non-stick baking parchment or Silpat.

This is going to get messy. Place a large sheet of baking parchment or cling film on your work surface and set up a bowl of caster sugar and a bowl of icing sugar, ready to roll the cookies. It helps if your hands are really cool. Run them under the cold tap or dip them in chilled water from time to time. You'll need to wash them quite frequently anyway, as it's a messy business.

Remove one batch of dough from the fridge at a time – you need it to be very cold when you work on it. Break off a small nugget of the dough about the size of a walnut and roll it quickly into a ball. Toss it first in the caster sugar then in the icing sugar until it's well coated, then place it on the baking sheet. Repeat, handling the dough as little as possible and placing the cookies about 3cm apart, until you've used up all the dough. Bake for 10–11 minutes, until the sugar coating

has split into a crackle pattern. Transfer them to a wire rack to cool completely – they will continue to firm up as they cool.

They will keep in an airtight container for about 4 days.

VARIATION

For an extra-luxe treat (because too much is never enough), chop some dark or milk chocolate into small shards of about 2g each and insert one into each cookie before rolling it in the sugars.

TIP

This dough freezes well, so you could keep the balls, before you roll them in the sugars, in the freezer ready for when you want to rustle up a quick batch.

~

Chapter 3

Accidentally Turkish

IF YOU'RE LOOKING FOR ME ON SUNDAY MORNING, I'd start at the Turkish Food Centre at the top of Ridley Road market in Dalston. After I've bought my flowers at Columbia Road market, I usually head there. Very occasionally I go to Chatsworth Road market too, but that seems rather unnecessarily like a triathlon and even I don't need organic churros, sourdough pizza or ninety-five kinds of kombucha that much. At least not before lunch.

Of course, TFC (we're friends, I'm allowed this familiarity) sells washing powder, loo roll and light bulbs like any normal supermarket, but that's not what brings me here.

Whenever I travel to a foreign country, I've barely unpacked my pants before I'm off to find the nearest supermarket. Trawling the aisles of condiments, tinned food and cleaning products is like a social anthropology field trip to me. What can you deduce about a country that has a dozen different kinds of ketchup, twenty varieties of tinned anchovies, or where their washing-up liquid is scented with raspberries and peach, rather than citrus? Let me give you my considered theories on that over the course of the next ninety pages. I will show . . .

OK, I won't, but I'm sure you know what I mean.

Strolling around the Turkish Food Centre is like a nano-holiday, except within minutes I can be in my own kitchen making lunch. I fill my inevitably wonky trolley with fistfuls of herbs, whole trays of tomatoes and peaches, bags of lemons, tubs of olives and feta, fresh from huge vats of brine, pillowy, still-warm flatbreads, links of *sucuk*, the spicy beef sausage, and bags of sweetly hot pul biber chilli, which I use almost as much as a condiment as an ingredient whenever I want to cheer a dish – or myself – up.

Usually, I'm not recreating Turkish recipes but, inspired by what I find, creating Turkish-ish dishes of my own. When I first moved to this part of London twenty-five years ago, I'd scan TFC's shelves for unfamiliar ingredients in alluring packaging and scribble down their names, before going home to look them up via my dial-up internet connection. This is how I introduced into my kitchen the everyday poetry of *kaymak*, *pekmez* and *kadayif*. That's clotted cream, fruit molasses and stringy pastry, possibly to you and certainly to me.

Whenever we're apart too long, I miss Hackney – my dearest, dirty, cranky and sometimes just plain weird belovèd. I miss being able to eat lunch whenever I want, a petition on every counter and a pop-up on every corner. I miss the bearded boys and the tattooed girls and being able to buy five different kinds of anything you like at midnight. And I definitely miss Turkish food. When I come home, I like to have breakfast at one of the many cafés on Stoke Newington High Street. In summer, I'll take the trad plate of olives, feta, tomatoes, cucumber, tomato, boiled egg, honey and a circle of chewy, sesame-encrusted *simit* bread. In winter, I choose *menemen*, that combination of green peppers, tomatoes and chillies with scrambled eggs and sometimes some added *sucuk*.

Even on cold days, I sit at a pavement table. This isn't just because I usually have my dogs with me, but because it's all the better to watch the neighbourhood theatre: the boys in the barber's having precise and elaborate patterns shaved into their hair, skateboarders whizzing past (cue my dog Barney: 'BARK BARK BARK YOU ARE MY MORTAL

ENEMY AND I WILL DESTROY YOU IN A MINUTE'), young couples with buggies, old ladies wheeling bags of laundry, the women in the flower shop arranging their pavement displays and old men absent-mindedly working colourful *tesbih*, or worry beads, through their fingers. If I'm really lucky, I might see a Turkish wedding – so much mascara, so much hair, so much satin, so many metres of ribbon looped into festive decoration on newly polished cars. And I count myself very lucky to call this home.

Turkish-ish grilled onion salad

SERVES ~ 4

This is my approximation of the free side salad they serve alongside your shish in many of the Turkish *ocakbaşi* restaurants on the Kingsland Road, Dalston's kebab heartlands and one of my favourite grocery shopping streets in the whole of London. The essential sourness comes from *şalgam suyu*, which translates as turnip water (but it's really juice from red carrot pickles flavoured with a bit of turnip). If you can't get your hands on a bottle, just use a few spoons of the juice from a jar of pickled gherkins. If you do get your hands on it, be aware that when served very cold it is a favourite Turkish hangover cure. Just passing that along. Hope it helps.

It may feel like a lot of herbs, but I promise it is not. They are an ingredient rather than a garnish and are essential to the vibrant character of the dish.

YOU WILL NEED . . . *Some metal skewers to grill the onions.*

3 medium yellow or white onions, about 500g, and 3 red onions, about the same weight

salt and freshly ground black pepper

4 tablespoons pomegranate molasses

4 tablespoons şalgam suyu or pickle juice

a good squeeze of lemon juice

2 cloves of garlic, halved, green germ removed, and very finely chopped

1 teaspoon chilli flakes

2 tablespoons olive oil, plus a little more for brushing

a big bunch of fresh flat-leaf parsley, about 30g, tough stalks removed, leaves and fine stalks chopped

1 bunch of fresh coriander, about 20g, tough stalks removed, leaves and fine stalks chopped

3 tablespoons roughly chopped fresh mint leaves

3 tablespoons roughly chopped fresh dill fronds

2 tablespoons toasted sesame seeds

TO SERVE
pillowy white bread

I sometimes make this on the barbecue. If you'd like to, start by lighting the grill – get the coals nice and hot, so they're glowing red underneath with a fine coating of grey ash on the top. Alternatively, just cook the onions under a very hot grill.

Peel the onions and cut them lengthways into 6 wedges, keeping the root intact so they don't fall apart. Thread them on to metal skewers, sprinkle with salt and place on a rack for 30 minutes. This not only helps season them but firms them up a little.

Whisk together the molasses, *şalgam suyu* or pickle juice, lemon juice, garlic, a good pinch of the chilli flakes from the 1 teaspoon, and olive oil to make a lovely, glossy dressing. Season with salt and pepper.

Brush the onions with olive oil, sprinkle a little more salt over them and grill for about 5–7 minutes per side, until gently charred around the edges. Carefully remove them from the skewers, snip off the roots, and toss them in the dressing. It seems like a lot of dressing – don't worry, you want lots so you can mop it up with chunks of bread.

Sprinkle the herbs over the onions with the sesame seeds and the rest of the chilli flakes, and toss together well. Serve warm or at room temperature.

~

Lamb and chickpea soup with minted yoghurt

SERVES ~ 6–8

I always slightly kick the furniture – metaphorically if not actually – when I have a cold and someone suggests chicken soup as the cure for all ills. Who is going to make this soup? Do the shopping and the preparing, and the general long, slow simmering of the soup? Wash the pan? The problem with invalid food is that it is often beyond the scope of the invalid. But the pestilent can't live on weak tea and hasty toast alone. When I am feeling sick or just tired, I often order in from Devran, a Turkish restaurant along the road from us, mostly because their food tastes like home cooking – they even have a casserole of the day. This soup is my version of their delicious and restorative lamb soup, which is balm to body and soul.

FOR THE SOUP

1kg lamb shoulder, cut into 3cm cubes

salt and freshly ground black pepper

2–3 tablespoons olive oil

2 medium onions, about 350g, diced

1 bay leaf

2 red peppers, halved, deseeded and cut into 1cm slices

4 cloves of garlic, halved, green germ removed, and very finely chopped

2 × 400g tins of chickpeas, drained and rinsed

2 teaspoons ground cumin

2 teaspoons ground coriander

—›

3 tablespoons biber salçasi *(or see* **TIP**, *page 43)*

800ml lamb, chicken or vegetable stock, or water

1 × 400g tin of chopped tomatoes

2 tablespoons red wine vinegar

2 teaspoons dried oregano

½ teaspoon pul biber, or a good pinch of chilli flakes

a large bunch of fresh parsley, about 20g, tough stalks removed and discarded, leaves and soft stalks chopped

a small bunch of fresh coriander, about 15g, tough stalks removed and discarded, leaves and soft stalks chopped

TO FINISH

about 160g Greek yoghurt

12–14 fresh mint leaves, chopped, or ½ teaspoon dried mint

a pinch of salt

Sprinkle 2 teaspoons of salt and 1 teaspoon of pepper over the lamb and mix it all together with your hands so that it is evenly seasoned. Warm the oil in a large, heavy-bottomed casserole or saucepan over a medium–high heat – you may not need all the oil, depending on how much fat remains on the lamb. Brown the lamb. You'll need to do this in batches, so as not to crowd the pan (see TIP, page 228). As pieces of the meat are well browned, remove them to a plate and continue until all the lamb is cooked.

When you have browned the meat, pour all but 3 tablespoons of fat from the pan (save it for frying bread or eggs – thank me later). Lower the heat, tip the onions into the pan with the bay leaf and sauté gently, stirring from time to time, until they are beautifully soft, about 20 minutes. Add the peppers and garlic and stir for 3–4 minutes, then stir in the chickpeas. Add the cumin and coriander and stir for a minute, then add the *biber salçasi* or pepper paste (see TIP opposite). Stir for a couple of minutes, then return the meat to the pan with any of the juices which have accumulated on the plate. Add the stock, tomatoes, vinegar, oregano and pul biber or chilli flakes. Bring to a very gentle simmer, then partially cover and let it blip away softly for an hour. Remove the lid, taste and add more salt and pepper if necessary, and simmer uncovered for 20–30 minutes, until the soup is thickened slightly and the lamb is very tender. Remove from the heat, fish out the bay leaf, and stir in the parsley and coriander.

In a small bowl, stir together the yoghurt, mint and salt. Serve the soup in warmed bowls, with some of the minted yoghurt spooned over the top.

TIP

Many Turkish recipes use an intense red pepper paste, *biber salçasi*. If you can't get hold of it, you can substitute a couple of jarred, drained flame-grilled red peppers – about 120g – whizzed together with 2 tablespoons of concentrated tomato purée, 2 teaspoons of paprika, ¼ teaspoon of cayenne and a pinch of cinnamon into a smooth paste. You can keep it sealed in a jar in the fridge for a couple of weeks and use it to perk up all manner of soups and stews – it is particularly good with aubergines.

~

Grilled pomegranate quail

SERVES ~ 6

There is a Turkish restaurant, Tas Firin, in Bethnal Green where every month or so I meet my friends Lucy and Lucy and Fi. We over-order, over-talk, and over-refresh on terrible wine. The waiters see us off into the night, our foil containers filled with leftovers still warm against our chests, with kind looks tinged – I'm not going to lie – slightly with relief. One of the dishes I always order is their grilled quail, eating it greedily with my fingers, between scandalous stories and unstoppable opinioning. This is my version, which you can cook under the grill or on the barbecue. I like the quail to be slightly pink in the middle – they can dry out very fast if you're not careful, as they are so small, so keep an eye on them.

Serve them with simple buttered rice, the grilled onion salad (see page 40) and flatbreads.

YOU WILL NEED . . .

Twelve 35cm metal skewers – you can usually fit one bird on two skewers (one through the legs, one through the breast). If you're using wooden skewers, soak them in water for a couple of hours so they don't burn while you're grilling. If you plan on a lot of barbecuing, keeping a bundle of soaked wooden skewers in the freezer means you always have some ready to go.

*6 quails, spatchcocked – get the butcher to do this for you if you're nervous, but it is honestly very simple to do yourself (see **TIP**, page 46). Courage!*

flaky sea salt

FOR THE MARINADE

70ml pomegranate molasses

juice of ½ a lemon

4 tablespoons olive oil

2 teaspoons pul biber (see page 38), or half chilli flakes, half paprika

2 teaspoons garlic powder

½ teaspoon salt

½ teaspoon ground cumin

¼ teaspoon ground cinnamon

TO FINISH

a handful of fresh coriander leaves; wedges of lemon; some pomegranate seeds; a bowl of Greek yoghurt, seasoned with salt and a good pinch of dried mint

Whisk together all the ingredients for the marinade in a large bowl, then add the quail and turn them over until they're well coated. Cover the bowl and refrigerate for 2–4 hours. Remove from the fridge an hour before grilling. Push a skewer through the legs of each quail, and another skewer through the wings and breast, ensuring they lie as flat as possible.

Line a grill tray with foil and preheat the grill until it's as hot as you can get it. You want to grill the birds about 10cm from the heating element. Grill the birds, bone side up, for 6–8 minutes, then turn and grill skin side up until the skin is slightly charred, a further 6–7 minutes, depending on the size of the quail. You may need to do this in batches, depending on how big your grill is.

To barbecue the birds . . . Wait until the coals are covered with a fine layer of grey ash and place the skewered birds on the medium–hot part of the grill, bone side down. Grill and rest as above, though check for doneness a couple of minutes before you would on your indoor grill.

Let the quail rest for 5 minutes before sprinkling them with flaky sea salt and arranging them on a platter over a mound of buttered rice, with the coriander leaves, lemon wedges and pomegranate seeds scattered over the top and the Greek yoghurt on the side.

TIP
To spatchcock the quails, place them breast side down. With poultry shears or sharp kitchen scissors, cut along either side of the backbones, remove the bones and offal and discard them.

~

Halva honey ice cream with sesame brittle

SERVES ~ 6–8

This is a very easy ice cream – no need to make an attention-seeking custard. Just whip together the mascarpone, cream and yoghurt and get cracking. The brittle isn't essential but it's a nice addition, a good crunchy contrast to the silky ice cream. And yes, you can make caramel. Hold your nerve.

FOR THE ICE CREAM
500g mascarpone
250g double cream
100g Greek yoghurt
80g runny honey, plus more
   for serving
1–2 teaspoons orange blossom
   water or rose water, depending
   on the strength

¼ teaspoon ground cardamom
150g plain halva, broken into pieces

FOR THE BRITTLE
vegetable oil, for greasing
150g caster sugar
3 tablespoons sesame seeds

Stir together the mascarpone, cream and yoghurt until smooth. Stir in 60g of the honey, the orange blossom water or rose water, and the cardamom. Churn in an ice cream maker, according to your machine's instructions (see TIP, page 49, if you don't have an ice cream maker). Scoop into a freezer-proof container. Use a spatula to stir through the halva and ripple through the remaining 20g of honey. Freeze for at least 3 hours before serving.

To make the brittle, line a baking sheet with lightly greased Silpat or non-stick baking parchment. Tip the sugar into a heavy-bottomed saucepan or frying pan. It's best to use a pan that has a pale interior so you can monitor the colour of the caramel easily. Warm the sugar over a medium heat. It will begin to melt – stir it a little with a wooden spoon to encourage it to melt evenly. Lower the heat a bit and leave to melt completely without stirring any more until the sugar is a rich, dark shade of amber. This should take about 5 minutes. Don't look away. Stir in the sesame seeds, then pour immediately on to the baking sheet. Leave to set and cool. Bash some into powder and break the rest into shards.

Serve the ice cream with some of the brittle powder and shards scattered over the top, and a last-minute trickle of honey.

TIP **HOW TO MAKE ICE CREAM WITHOUT AN ICE CREAM MAKER**

I love to make ice cream and sorbets, and I loved to make them long before I had a machine to help me, so if you don't have an ice cream maker, don't let that put you off. Pour the chilled ice cream mixture into a shallow, freezer-proof container, cover it and put it into the freezer. After 45 minutes, take it out and use a rubber spatula to drag into the middle the bits around the edges that are beginning to freeze. Give everything a really good stir and return it to the freezer. Leave it for 30 minutes or so and repeat. You'll probably have to do this two or three more times as it freezes. The end results won't be quite as smooth as if you were using a machine, but you will have ice cream and it will be delicious.

Chapter 4

How to throw a party without losing your mind

LET ME TELL YOU ABOUT THE WORST PARTY I EVER THREW. Strictly speaking, it was a series of parties. I fully committed. Gather round, children, for this terrible story of yore.

It was the first Christmas after Séan and I were married and I had somehow spun myself into a Hallmark Channel-esque frenzy of cable knits, needlepoint stockings on the fireplace and a tree that would shame the good people of Norway with their paltry Trafalgar Square offering. All this in a two-bed flat in Hackney. My levels of control-freakery were unfettered, some might say unhinged, and I had cupboards full of wedding china and glassware desperately in need of their first airing.

So this is what I did. I organized a drinks party for the neighbours on Christmas Eve, before running off to midnight mass at St Mary's with my parents. The next morning I inflicted on us all a choreographed-to-the-minute champagne, smoked salmon and scrambled egg breakfast, followed by the full jingle-bells-and-whistles Christmas lunch for a dozen or so of our family, and then, because too much is never enough, an afternoon tea on Boxing Day for those who couldn't be with us on Christmas Day.

Everything homemade. From scratch. Like a lunatic. Did I think I was the only person in the country who owned a dining table?

My friend Lola has an absolute aversion to 'showing off'. It is honestly the very worst criticism she can make about a person. And while I think with feeding people we all crave that taaa-daaaaah! moment when we bring something delicious to the table (cooking: showbiz for greedy people), I think she may be on to something.

My demented Mama Claus act taught me this: my ego got in the way of a good time and it is most definitely not what the Baby Jesus – nor my poor guests – would have wanted. Not one person who spent Christmas with us would have cared if we'd eaten bought mince pies and drunk cheap fizz as we slummocked about in our pyjamas watching *Home Alone*. I learned that if you're enjoying yourself, everyone else will enjoy themselves too. Nothing tastes as good as happy feels. This revelation was the Christmas miracle I will carry in my heart forever.

Since then, I have thrown hundreds of lunches, dinners, cocktail parties and big events. I've catered other people's parties and weddings, and these are the things I have learned.

Do things for love or money, never out of a sense of obligation or to ingratiate yourself with people you think might be useful (they can always, always tell, and also it leads to the worst kind of showing off). Only accept invitations from people who you would be happy to have in your own home, or the guilt of not returning the favour will gnaw at you in an entirely undelicious way.

I love to make lists, lovely soothing lists. Writing down recipe ideas, shopping lists, cooking times, serving ideas, makes me feel, briefly, like the queen of the universe. When you cook for people you love, however simply, however extravagantly, you create your own contained world where the worst that can happen is a split sauce.

You know your own kitchen better than I do. You know how much you can have on the hob or in the oven at the same time, which ring burns hot, which part of the grill cooks unevenly, but more importantly, you know your own levels of skill and comfort. This is not to discourage you from being ambitious, from trying new and complex things, just don't try them all at once after work on a rainy Tuesday night in November.

My own blueprint for an easy dinner is to lay out some platters of charcuterie, bowls of olives, salted Marcona almonds and other antipasti for when everyone arrives, to stave off hunger and drunkenness, particularly if you have late arrivals. I seldom do a sit-down starter, preferring the happy buzz of people chatting in the kitchen as I cook, but I sometimes do something simple and hot to pass around, such as salt and pepper squid or sautéd Padrón peppers, because a little bit of sizzle is a good and cheerful thing. As a main course, I love something generous which I can make ahead, like the duck Parmentier here (page 60). And I never tire of a roast chicken (page 56). Roast chicken is my love language. If I have lots of people, I just make a few of them and lay them out along the table like some sort of banquet for a medieval merchant. I might make a couple of generous vegetable dishes, but it's important to remember not everything has to dance on the piano, not everything has to be 'a recipe'. Sometimes all you need is some buttered green beans, roast potatoes (never wrong) or a green salad (page 27). This kind of simplicity is far preferable to lots of complicated sides, which leave you exhausted and your guests overwhelmed. Oh yes, and when it comes to serving, go easy. You can spend hours cooking only to ruin it at the last minute by piling the plates so high that things smoosh horribly together, imbuing your efforts with all the appeal of the compost bin. I much prefer to spoon a smaller amount on to the plates, then lay the serving dishes down the middle of the table so people can help themselves to more if they want.

I'd like to say something about delegation: do it. The most obvious benefit is that it takes some of the burden off your shoulders, particularly if you're hosting alone. Rope someone in to lay the table (I always get Séan to do this, ever since he watched a documentary about a state banquet at Buckingham Palace where the butlers measured the distance of the cutlery from the edge of the table with a ruler and he said, 'Isn't that a good idea?' Before he even finished the sentence, he had inadvertently got himself a job for life).

Get someone else to set up the drinks if you can, and make sure there's plenty of ice, mixers, soft drinks, sliced fruit, herbs, all that is required to pixie up a simple gin and tonic into a treat. That said, you are not the American Bar at the Savoy. Something sparkling, a white, a light red, a rosé in summer, the makings of one, maximum two, cocktails is quite enough (NB No showing off). I once interviewed the formidable Australian domestic dynamo Donna Hay, and she gave me this great tip. Write or print a recipe for a simple cocktail and lay out all that's required to make it beautifully. Let your guests help themselves.

Speaking of which, delegation not only frees you to commit acts of culinary genius, it can be an enormous benefit to others too. If you're inviting new people or have a shy guest, getting them to help serve drinks or pass round platters of salami is a great way to get everyone talking without awkwardness or descending into that absolute social null of discussing how you got there and where you parked. (PS Never discuss this. I would genuinely rather talk about sex and death.)

I have told you all this, but I could have stopped ages ago (I know I didn't, I like a chat), and just told you this: mostly your friends don't care what you put in front of them, unless it is actively poisonous. If all anyone's talking about the next day is the food, you haven't really got it right. I want them to be talking about new friends they've made, or who fell off a chair laughing. I want loud conversation and to be dancing around the kitchen to old vinyl. I want a little scandal and a lot of fun. And all that takes – in the kitchen as in life – is for you to make your plans, hope for the best, and whatever happens, keep going.

The roast chicken that goes with everything

SERVES ~ 4–6, depending on what you serve alongside it. If I'm expecting a lot
of people, I often roast two or three at a time

When in doubt, roast a chicken. When you're sad or happy, when the sun is
shining or it's raining outside, roast a chicken. When you have family coming, or
new friends over for dinner, you know what to do. I love roast chicken so much,
it's often my 'What shall I make?' lunch or dinner, with a salad and some roast
potatoes. Also, there is no aroma in the world as breathe-out-all-will-be-well as
the smell of a buttery, garlicky, herby roasted chicken wafting through the house.
If I love you, this is what I will cook for you.

1 large chicken, about 2kg

salt and freshly ground black pepper

1 unwaxed lemon, cut into quarters
lengthways

1 small bunch of fresh thyme and/or
tarragon

1 bay leaf

120g unsalted butter, room
temperature

4 cloves of garlic, halved, green germ
removed, and very finely chopped

1 teaspoon chopped fresh thyme
leaves, or 1 tablespoon chopped
fresh tarragon, or both

finely grated zest of 1 small unwaxed
lemon, grated straight on to the
butter

1 tablespoon lemon juice

FOR THE TIN

1 large-ish carrot, about 70g,
quartered lengthways

1 large onion, about 300g, cut into
thick slices

1 bulb of garlic, halved horizontally

2 bay leaves

a few sprigs of thyme

450ml white wine

450ml chicken stock

Preheat the oven to 220°C/200°C/gas 7.

Season the inside of the bird with salt and pepper, then put the lemon
wedges and whole herbs in the cavity. You don't need to truss it, other than for
neatness if that is your thing. Untrussed, it will cook more quickly.

In a small bowl, mash together 80g of the butter with the garlic, chopped
herbs, lemon zest and juice, and season with ½ teaspoon each of salt and pepper.
Gently push your fingers under the skin on the breast of the bird, either side of
the bone, being careful not to tear it. Push the butter under the skin and massage it
into the flesh so it spreads out a bit.

Place the carrot, onion and garlic bulb (cut side up) in the centre of a small roasting tin (see TIP) with the bay leaves and thyme sprigs – you want them to act as a sort of trivet for the bird – and put the chicken on top. Rub the remaining 40g of butter into the skin, then season very generously with salt and pepper – probably more generously than you think you need to.

Put the bird into the oven and roast for 1 hour 10 minutes, basting once at about 40 minutes. Check that the juices run clear when you pierce the flesh between leg and thigh with a sharp knife – there should be no hint of pink. If you need to, put it back into the oven and test every 5 minutes for doneness. Remove it from the oven and put the chicken on a warm plate covered in foil to rest for 15 minutes while you make the gravy.

Put the roasting tin on the hob over a lowish heat, pour in the wine and stir vigorously, scraping up any brown bits on the bottom of the pan. Let it bubble away for a minute or two, then strain it into a pan and continue to simmer until it is reduced to a third of its original volume. You can discard the vegetable trivet now, but you may want to squeeze some of the roasted garlic into the pan with the reduced wine. Add the stock and simmer for 5 minutes or so to intensify the flavour. Season with salt and pepper if you need to – this will depend on how heavily seasoned the chicken is – and serve in a warmed jug.

TIP

If you can, the day before you want to cook your chicken, remove all its packaging, pat it dry with kitchen paper, then place it in a small roasting tin and return it to the fridge. This helps dry out the skin so it will crisp up beautifully when you cook it. Take the chicken out of the fridge an hour before you want to roast it. By using a tin into which the chicken fits cosily, it means that the juices and fat can accumulate in the bottom of the tin to help you make delicious gravy, rather than becoming a burnt-on mess as it does if it spreads itself thinly in a large tin.

Duck Parmentier

SERVES ~ **8–10**

I often serve this on New Year's Eve as it's so easy to make for a crowd – the recipe doubles and triples up beautifully, depending on how many guests you have – and it's rich and profoundly satisfying, so a little goes a long way. Also, it has near-miraculous booze-soaking-up properties, if it's that kind of night. I serve it simply, with buttered green beans.

4 confit legs of duck, one large tin usually

4 medium onions, about 700g, halved and cut into thin slices

3 torpedo shallots, about 210g, halved and cut into thin slices

3 sprigs of fresh thyme

salt and freshly ground black pepper

150ml red wine

3 tablespoons red wine vinegar

20g finely chopped parsley leaves

1.2kg floury potatoes, such as King Edwards or Bintje, peeled and cut into large, equal-sized chunks

150ml crème fraîche

90g unsalted butter

¼ teaspoon freshly grated nutmeg

10g fresh white breadcrumbs

Place the duck legs in a bowl over a pan of barely simmering water to melt the fat. Reserve 3 tablespoons of the fat to fry the onions and shallots and tip the rest into a jar. Keep the jar in the fridge, to use for your roast potatoes and fried eggs, and generally to make you happy. Remove the duck legs from the bowl and shred them roughly into pieces. You don't want them too small – they will break up as they cook anyway.

Warm the 3 tablespoons of duck fat in a large, heavy-bottomed saucepan over a medium–low heat, add the onions and shallots with the thyme sprigs and a generous pinch of salt, and fry gently, stirring now and again until softened and beginning to turn golden, about 40 minutes. Don't skimp at this stage. It makes all the difference to the final flavour. Add the shredded duck, raise the heat a little and fry until the duck is heated through. Add the wine and vinegar and simmer for 5 minutes, gently stirring from time to time. Remove the thyme sprigs, stir in the parsley, season well with salt and pepper and spoon into an ovenproof dish, approximately 30 × 20 × 8cm. You can make this part of the Parmentier a day or two ahead, just keep it covered in the fridge.

Next, make the mashed potatoes. Bring a large pan of well-salted water to the boil and add the potatoes. Cook them until tender, then drain them. Leave them in the colander to steam for a few minutes. Preheat the oven to 200°C/180°C fan/gas 6.

Tip the potatoes back into the pan and mash them well, or pass them through a potato ricer. With a wooden spoon, beat in the crème fraîche and two-thirds of the butter until smooth. Add the nutmeg, taste and season well. Spoon the potatoes over the top of the duck and rough up the surface with a fork. Sprinkle on the breadcrumbs and dot with the remaining butter. Place the dish on a baking sheet and cook for 35 minutes, until the top is golden and the filling bubbling.

~

Green and black salad

SERVES ~ 6–8, depending what you are serving alongside it

Several years ago, I was invited to a cookery lesson with Harumi Kurihara to launch her latest recipe book. A dozen or so journalists gathered hungrily in the teaching kitchen of the Divertimenti cookware shop on Marylebone High Street. Harumi was introduced to us by her publisher as the Japanese Martha Stewart, someone so famous she was known by her first name only. She made half a dozen beautiful dishes, including a salad of green beans dressed with black sesame seeds, mirin and soy sauce. It was so simple and striking – as though the brilliant emerald beans had been tossed in volcanic sand – I have used and adapted the dressing ever since, on all kinds of raw, steamed and roasted vegetables.

When it's in season, I often add a couple of handfuls of that superfine asparagus to this salad too, the sort that's as thin as the thinnest pencil.

FOR THE SALAD
500g fine green beans

300g frozen petits pois

300g frozen edamame beans, or frozen skinned broad beans

FOR THE DRESSING
50g black sesame seeds

juice of a lime (see **TIP**, *page 212)*

3 tablespoons soy sauce

2 tablespoons mirin

1 tablespoon caster sugar

TO FINISH
a handful of coriander, fine stems and leaves, about 15g, roughly chopped

10–12 mint leaves, roughly chopped

Fill a large bowl with iced water. Bring two pans of water to the boil. In one, simmer the green beans for 2–3 minutes until just tender. Tip the petits pois and edamame beans or broad beans into the second pan, cover and bring back to the boil and simmer for 2 minutes. Drain all the vegetables and plunge them into the iced water to stop them cooking further. Drain and pat dry with kitchen paper or on a clean tea towel.

To make the dressing, warm a small frying pan over a medium heat and gently toast the sesame seeds for a couple of minutes until just fragrant. Either in a food processor or with a mini chopper, grind or pulse the sesame seeds – you don't want them to be a paste, just break them up a bit to help release their flavour. Mix well with the rest of the dressing ingredients. In a large bowl, mix all the

vegetables with the dressing. I like to do this with my hands, which is rather ghoulish but satisfying. Turn out on a platter to serve, scattered with the coriander and mint.

~

My favourite potato salad

SERVES ~ 6–10, depending on what else you are serving alongside it

My own potato salad adheres strictly to my belief that two good things are invariably better than one good thing, so yes please to both vinaigrette and mayonnaise. I dress the still-warm potatoes in a sharp, mustardy vinaigrette and leave them to cool completely before cracking on with the rest. Then I toss the potatoes with celery, cucumber and gherkins, spring onions, peas, boiled eggs and parsley, before folding it all in a combination of mayonnaise and thick yoghurt spiked with a little more mustard. Sometimes I add capers, and sometimes I vary the herbs – tossing in some chives, chervil and/or tarragon along with the parsley. If I'm making it the day before – and I usually am – I add the herbs and the onion when I give it a last stir, about an hour before serving. To me, it's the essence of pure contentment and pleasure: easy, comforting, to be enjoyed in big, heaped spoonfuls on summer plates, but also – with any luck – there will always be enough left over for me to enjoy on late-night solitary forages through the fridge, when it often tastes the most delicious of all.

FOR THE SALAD

1.2kg waxy potatoes, such as Anya or Yukon Gold, peeled and halved, or quartered if huge

170g petits pois or garden peas, fresh or frozen

1 celery stick, trimmed (and if at all tough, slide a sharp vegetable peeler over the ribbed surface to destring it – it really is worth it, I promise), then finely diced

½ a cucumber, about 180g, cut into 1cm dice

30g cornichons or gherkins, chopped

15g capers, rinsed

*6 hard-boiled eggs (see **TIP**, page 66)*

4 spring onions, trimmed and finely sliced

a big handful of fresh parsley, leaves and fine stems, about 20g, roughly chopped

FOR THE VINAIGRETTE

3 tablespoons white wine vinegar

2½ tablespoons Dijon mustard

½ teaspoon salt

a few grinds of black pepper

140ml mild olive oil

FOR THE DRESSING

70g mild mayonnaise, such as Hellmann's

70g thick Greek yoghurt

1 tablespoon Dijon or wholegrain mustard – I like to use wholegrain here, for the pretty seeds

salt and freshly ground black pepper

First, cook the potatoes. Put them into a pan of salted water, bring to the boil, then simmer until tender when pierced with a small, sharp knife, about 10–12 minutes. (While they're boiling, make the vinaigrette as described below.) Drain the potatoes in a colander and let them steam for a few minutes to lose some of their moisture.

In the bottom of a large bowl, whisk together the vinegar, mustard, salt and pepper, then slowly trickle in the oil, whisking as you go, until it's thickened and glossy. Gently toss the still-warm potatoes in the dressing and leave to cool completely. You can do this the day before you want to serve it if you like, just cover and refrigerate them.

Cook the peas in a pan of boiling water, or steam them – 2 minutes for petits pois, 3 minutes for garden peas. When cooked, rinse under very cold water to stop them cooking further and losing their colour, or plunge them into a bowl of iced water.

Toss together the potatoes, peas, celery, cucumber, cornichons and capers. Roughly chop 4 of the eggs (reserve the rest to put on the top at the end) and gently fold them in.

In a small bowl, stir together the mayonnaise, yoghurt and mustard. Taste and season with salt and pepper, then spoon it over the potato salad and gently toss everything together with a rubber spatula until well combined. Cover it and refrigerate for 4 hours or overnight for all the flavours to blend. Remove from the fridge an hour before serving. Toss with the spring onions, most of the parsley and any other herbs you might be using. Quarter the remaining eggs and arrange them over the top of the potato salad, along with a generous scattering of parsley.

TIP **HOW TO BOIL AN EGG**

I just do what Delia says. It's usually for the best. Place the eggs in a small pan – just large enough to hold them without them touching and jostling each other. Add cool water, enough to cover them by about 1cm, then bring to the boil, lower to a simmer and cook for 6 minutes – this will give you a hard-boiled egg that is still slightly soft in the middle, which is what you want. Drain and run them under cold water for at least a minute, or put them into a bowl of iced water to cool completely. This stops them developing that grim grey ring around the yolk.

~

Lemony roast cauliflower, with almonds and curd cheese

SERVES ~ 10-ish as a side dish, depending on what else you are serving with it

I love this combination of spiced, roast cauliflower, zingy lemon and sweet, sticky Medjool dates. It's great as part of a large spread with other salads, but feel free to halve the quantities for smaller groups, or for mid-week dinners – it's really delicious with lamb chops, or the grilled pomegranate quail (see page 44).

80ml extra virgin olive oil, plus more for dressing

finely grated zest and juice of 2 unwaxed lemons

2 tablespoons ground cumin

1 tablespoon ground coriander

½ teaspoon paprika

¼ teaspoon ground cinnamon

2 large cauliflowers, about 800g each, broken into medium-sized florets, leaves reserved for the deliciousness (see TIP, page 68)

salt and freshly ground black pepper

200g farro

chicken or vegetable stock (this can be from a stock cube or pot)

150g flaked almonds

100g Medjool dates, stoned and roughly chopped

3 preserved lemons, halved, pips discarded, diced

30g fresh parsley leaves and fine stalks, coarsely chopped

20g fresh coriander leaves and fine stalks, coarsely chopped

TO FINISH

150g curd cheese (see page 74) or ricotta

finely grated zest of 1 unwaxed lemon

Preheat the oven to 220°C/200°C fan/gas 7. Line two large baking trays with non-stick baking parchment or Silpat.

In a large bowl, whisk together the olive oil, lemon zest and juice, cumin, ground coriander, paprika and cinnamon. Tip in the cauliflower florets and mix well, so everything is coated. I find it easiest to do this with my immaculately clean hands.

Scatter the cauliflower evenly over the prepared baking trays, season with salt and pepper, and roast for 30–35 minutes, turning once or twice, until they are tender and beginning to char around the edges. (While they're cooking, there are other things to do, so don't nod off.) If you're going to use the leaves (see below), add them about 10 minutes into the cooking time.

While the cauliflowers are roasting, cook the farro. Rinse it well, bring a pan of well-flavoured stock to the boil and simmer the farro for 25–30 minutes until it's cooked but still has a little bite to it. Drain it and leave it to steam and dry out slightly in a colander.

In a large frying pan over a medium heat, toast the flaked almonds until they are just beginning to become fragrant and golden, about 3–4 minutes, rattling the pan frequently.

When the cauliflower is cooked, spoon it into a large bowl and toss it with the farro, almonds, dates, preserved lemons and herbs, saving some of the herbs and almonds to sprinkle over the top to finish. If you're using the leaves, add them now too. Taste and add more salt and pepper if you think it needs it.

Arrange the salad on a large serving platter, scatter over the remaining herbs and almonds, dot with the curd cheese or ricotta, grate over the lemon zest and trickle on some olive oil just before serving.

TIP WHAT TO DO WITH THE LEAVES?

First of all, do not throw those squeaky, magnificent leaves away. Sometimes they take up most of the cauliflower and it's a terrible shame to waste them. Chop the biggest ones into 4cm chunks and keep the smaller, more tender leaves whole. Toss them in olive oil, sprinkle them with salt and roast them at 220°C/200°C fan/gas 7 for about 15–20 minutes, turning once, until the thick stems are tender and the leaves are beginning to char. You can serve them mixed in with this salad, or on their own at another meal.

~

Chapter 5

Busy doing nothing: the weekend kitchen

ONE OF THE MOST STEALTHILY DELIGHTFUL THINGS ABOUT COOKING is that it can be our ally in sloth. It's the finest way I know of looking busy while doing almost nothing. Could I pick up that parcel from the post office? Bath the dog? Go to that deadly yet improving lecture? No, sorry, I'm cooking. It's the ultimate get-out-of-tedium-free card.

I am by nature enormously lazy but by birth, northern. These qualities conflict with each other, one requiring extensive sofa privileges and the other, relentless hard graft. The kitchen is where I can make these strange bedfellows best friends.

During the week, I play To-do List Jenga. Hard frying, pressure cooking, quickly assembling, finger-burning haste takes the place of slow simmering, gentle stirring and just letting things be themselves and seeing what happens. So at weekends, or honestly whenever I can, holing up in the kitchen, pottering about, is my yoga, my wellness break, my Zen. There is great, quiet joy to be had in letting things take the time they take.

In family legend, as a child I loved the seaside and spent hours, bottom in the air, gazing into rock pools, running my fingers through the salt water and decanting tiny crabs and sea urchins into bright plastic buckets. Hours. And that's how I feel now when I'm in the kitchen. I tie on an apron, pull out some pans, grab a wooden spoon and then four hours have passed, or five, or six. I have chopped and stirred and tasted. I have listened to a whole book on Audible or half-watched a dozen episodes of something trashy on Netflix, or learned something I never knew, and never knew I wanted to know until now, from Radio 4.

This kind of pottering-about cooking takes two forms. The first is creating useful and delicious things which will add ease, savour and elegance to the following days, such as the pickled grapes to go with cheese (page 73), or the versatile curd cheese (page 74), which I crumble over salads and roasted vegetables, or use in open sandwiches. Jams, terrines, cured things, pickled things, things in jars and bottles, or wrapped in waxed paper – in short, anything Ma from *Little House on the Prairie* might cheerfully place in the Ingalls' larder, to brighten another day. The second kind of bounty invariably produced – if that doesn't sound too much like hard work – on kitchen-pottering days is those entirely trivial and life-affirming things, often sweet, which are just for right now, to make *this* moment better, sweeter, more precious. Cakes, pies, biscuits, scones and puddings, gone in less time than it takes to say their names, but each honouring the day of their creation as a special one. Just get someone else to bath the dog.

Pickled grapes

MAKES ~ **1 × 1-litre jar**

I mostly make these to go with cheese – I love them particularly with Roquefort and soft, creamy goat's cheese, but they are very good with roast pork, pâtés and terrines too, or as an ingredient in a pear, endive, blue cheese and toasted walnut salad.

600g black grapes

400ml cider vinegar

200ml white wine

300g light muscovado sugar

1 teaspoon salt

1 rosemary branch, about 5cm long

12 juniper berries

½ teaspoon peppercorns

Sterilize a large jar (see page 79) with a vinegar-proof lid and warm it gently in a low oven while you get on with the rest.

Remove the grapes from their stems and rinse them well. Leave them to dry on kitchen paper or on a clean tea towel.

Put the vinegar and wine into a saucepan large enough to hold all the liquid and the grapes. Tip in the sugar and warm over a medium heat, stirring until it dissolves, then add the salt, rosemary, juniper and peppercorns and simmer for a minute. Drop in the grapes, put the lid on to bring it quickly to the boil, and simmer for a further minute. Don't boil any longer than that or the skins will start slipping off.

With a slotted spoon, put the grapes into the warm jar, packing them in as tightly as you can. Pour over the hot liquid, tucking in the aromatics and making sure everything is completely covered with the liquid. Seal the jar and store for a couple of weeks before eating. Once open, store in the fridge and eat within a couple of weeks.

~

Herby lemony curd cheese

MAKES ~ about 250–300g, depending on how thick you want it

There is nothing like having a sieve lined with muslin nestled over a bowl to induce that happy homesteader *Little House on the Prairie* feeling. I make curd cheese a lot, especially if I have milk or cream that's about to turn and needs using up. I use it in salads, serve it for breakfast, dot it over roast vegetables. Its uses are almost endless. Just make sure absolutely everything is scrupulously, squeakily clean – pan, spoons, sieve, muslin, hands. The curd cheese keeps quite well in the fridge for 3–5 days, getting slightly riper as it matures.

1 litre whole milk, or 750ml whole milk and 250ml double cream

½ teaspoon salt

3 tablespoons lemon juice, white wine vinegar or cider vinegar

Pour the milk, or the milk and cream, into a saucepan with the salt and warm it over a medium heat, stirring gently. Just as bubbles appear around the edge, add the lemon or vinegar and let it steam very gently on the heat for a minute. Remove the pan from the hob and let it sit for 15 minutes for the curds to separate from the whey.

Line a large sieve with some muslin, scalded with boiling water from the kettle and wrung out. Pour the curds and whey into the sieve. Leave it to drain for 35 minutes to an hour – the longer you leave it, the thicker it will get. Gently squeeze the muslin to remove a little more whey, then tip the curd cheese into a container.

Season it with lemon zest, lemon thyme leaves, chilli flakes, cumin, anything you like really, or enjoy it with honey for breakfast. Don't throw out the whey – use it in bread or pancakes.

~

Rhubarb, rosewater and vanilla jam

MAKES ~ **3 × 370g jars**

Rhubarb is low in pectin, so even when using jam sugar you won't get a strong set. I don't mind that it's a softer jam – its colour is incredibly beautiful and it's delicious with buttermilk scones (see page 79) or spooned over Greek yoghurt.

700g jam sugar, with pectin

700g rhubarb, trimmed weight, cut into 2.5cm chunks

1 vanilla pod

2 blood oranges, or smallish oranges

1 small lemon

1–2 tablespoons rose water

Tip a layer of sugar into the bottom of a preserving pan or large stainless steel pan and add a layer of rhubarb. Split the vanilla pod lengthways with a small, sharp knife. Scrape out the seeds and dot them over the rhubarb; lay the pod on top. Continue layering the sugar and rhubarb, finishing with a layer of sugar.

Juice the oranges – you should have about 100ml of juice – and the lemon. Pour the juice over the rhubarb, cover the pan and leave it overnight to macerate.

The next day, place a couple of saucers in the freezer and sterilize your jars (see TIP, page 79). Warm the jam gently, stirring it slowly from time to time to dissolve the sugar without breaking up the pieces of rhubarb. Once the sugar has dissolved (see TIP, page 79), bring to a rolling boil and boil rapidly until the setting point is reached, which should take about 8–10 minutes. This is a soft-set jam, so don't expect it to get too solid. After cooling for a minute, a droplet of the jam on one of the chilled saucers should just wrinkle when you push it with your finger – it won't be as strong a wrinkle as you get with some jams, more a gentle furrow.

Remove the pan from the heat and let it sit for 5 minutes. Stir in the rose water. Judge for yourself how strong you would like that flavour to be. I am very much a 2 tablespoon person, but you may be a more subtle type than I am. Either discard the vanilla pod – you can rinse it, let it dry out and add it to your jar of vanilla sugar if you like (see page 182) – or snip a little bit into each warm, sterilized jar. Ladle the jam into the jars. Fill to the brim and immediately seal with the lids. Turn the jars upside down for a minute – this helps to ensure the lid is sealed – then turn them the right way up and leave to cool. Label the jars and date them. You think you'll remember but you won't. Unopened and kept in a cool, dark place the jam should keep for a year. Once opened, keep it in the fridge and use within a month.

~

Peach and raspberry jam

MAKES ~ 3 × 370g jars

This is a soft-set, summery jam which is beautiful on scones, used to sandwich together a Victoria sponge or stirred into yoghurt. All in all, a very good use of your time.

600g peaches

800g jam sugar, with pectin

juice of 1 lemon

500g raspberries

small knob of unsalted butter, about 5g

1 tablespoon Grand Marnier or Cointreau (optional)

Bring a small pan of water to the boil and fill a bowl with iced water. Cut a small cross in the bottom of the peaches with a sharp knife. Use tongs to lower each peach one at a time into the boiling water for 20 seconds, then plunge them into the iced water. The skins should slip off easily; I sometimes just rub them off with a sheet of kitchen paper. Halve them and remove the stones, then cut the peaches into 2cm pieces.

Put the peaches into a preserving pan or a large stainless steel pan and sprinkle on the sugar and the lemon juice. Stir gently, cover and leave to macerate for 4 hours or overnight, stirring a couple of times. Put a couple of saucers into the freezer and prepare some sterilized jars (see TIP, page 79).

Warm the pan over a medium heat, stirring until the sugar has dissolved (see TIP, page 79). Add the raspberries, stir, and bring to a strong, rolling boil. Test for a setting point after 8–10 minutes – drop a teaspoon of jam on a chilled saucer, leave for a minute, and then it should wrinkle when you push it with your finger. If it doesn't, test every 2 minutes until you get a set. Remove the pan from the heat. Skim off any foam and stir in the butter, which will help to dissolve any of the remaining bubbles. Leave to cool for 5 minutes, then stir in the Grand Marnier or Cointreau if you are using it. Ladle the jam into the hot jars – a jam funnel helps. Fill to the brim and immediately seal with the lids. Turn the jars upside down for a minute – this helps to ensure the lid is sealed – then turn the right way up and leave to cool. When you label the jars, make sure you include the date. The jam will keep for up to a year in a cool, dry place. When opened, keep it in the fridge and use within a month.

If you stir the jam and you still see crystals of sugar clinging to the sides of the pan, or the spoon is at all 'gritty', keep warming it gently until all the crystals disappear. Then you can bring it to a very brisk boil.

HOW TO STERILIZE JARS

With preserving, hygiene is all. Make sure all your equipment is scrupulously clean and your hands would pass a strict matron's inspection. Wash the jars in hot, soapy water and rinse them well, or run them through the dishwasher. When you're almost ready to use them, put them on a tray in a 140°C/120°C fan/gas 1 oven for at least 15 minutes, so they are warm when you add the jam.

Buttermilk lemon scones

MAKES ~ **12 scones**

These are tender and delicate scones. It's essential to work quickly and gently, to coax them into lightness. They are incredibly good with one of the jams in this chapter, either simply with butter or with clotted cream.

400g self-raising flour, plus a little more for dusting

1 teaspoon baking powder

½ teaspoon salt

100g very cold unsalted butter, cut into small cubes

50g caster sugar

finely grated zest of 1 small, unwaxed lemon (see the recipe for advice on how to get the most out of your lemon)

280ml pot of buttermilk

Preheat the oven to 220°C/200°C fan/gas 7. Line a baking sheet with Silpat or non-stick baking parchment.

Put the flour, baking powder and salt into a bowl and whisk them all together. Briskly rub the butter into the flour with your fingertips until it resembles coarse crumbs, with a few little nuggets of butter left in the mixture. Whisk in the sugar. Using the fine side of a box grater or a Microplane grater, grate the lemon zest directly into the bowl – this ensures you don't lose any of the fragrant citrus oil. Be careful not to grate in any bitter white pith.

Reserve 3 tablespoons of the buttermilk in a small bowl.

Make a well in the middle of the flour mixture and pour in the buttermilk. With a dinner knife, quickly work it into a sticky dough. Turn it out on to a lightly floured surface or on to some cling film dusted with flour, and gently coax it into a circle. Roll it out with a floured rolling pin until it is 2cm thick. Dip a 6cm round pastry cutter into some flour and begin to cut out your scones, placing them quite close together on the prepared baking sheet as you go. Gently press together any scraps and continue cutting until you have used up the dough. Brush the tops of the scones with the reserved buttermilk and place them in the oven to bake until they lift easily from the baking sheet and are golden on the top, about 13–15 minutes.

ALTERNATIVE
Instead of the lemon zest, add 2 teaspoons of vanilla extract with the buttermilk.

TIP
If you can't find buttermilk, either do what Johann suggests (page 269) and mix some yoghurt with a generous splash of lemon juice, or add a squeeze of lemon to whole milk and let it stand for 5 minutes before using it.

Cheddar, chive and Marmite scones

MAKES ~ **6 scones**

My friend, food writer Thane Prince, introduced me to adding Marmite to scones and honestly I have never looked back. Even if you're not a fan of Marmite, do give it a try, as it adds a wonderfully rounded savouriness. And if you are a fan, serve the scones still warm, split, with plenty of butter and a little more Marmite for good luck. The slightly rough-puff folding technique I use here ensures light and flaky scones, which is what you want. The secret is to go gently and work the dough as little as possible. I like to use a square cutter for savoury scones, to differentiate them on the tea table from sweet ones, but it really doesn't matter if you only have a round cutter – use that!

250g self-raising flour, plus a little more for rolling out and dusting the cutter

1 teaspoon baking powder

1 teaspoon English mustard powder

½ teaspoon salt

50g unsalted butter, very cold, cut into small cubes

1 tablespoon finely chopped chives

2 teaspoons Marmite

160ml whole milk

100g coarsely grated Cheddar cheese

a little milk or single cream for brushing the tops

Preheat the oven to 200°C/180°C fan/gas 6. Line a baking sheet with Silpat or non-stick baking parchment.

Put the flour, baking powder, mustard powder and salt into a bowl and whisk them together, or sieve them into the bowl if you don't already have enough to do. Briskly rub the butter into the flour with your fingertips until it resembles coarse crumbs, with a few little nuggets of butter left in the mixture. Sprinkle on the chives and stir. In a small jug, whisk the Marmite into the milk until it is well blended.

Make a well in the flour mixture and stir in the milk using a dinner knife, until you have a soft, craggy dough. Turn it out on to a floured surface, or on to floured cling film or parchment if you're worried about it sticking, and pat together gently into a round. With a floured pin, roll out to a rectangle, approximately 21 × 14cm. Sprinkle two-thirds of the cheese on top, then fold it over itself twice, like folding a letter (remember those?), and roll out again to 2cm thick. Dip a square 7cm cutter into flour, then cut out the scones and place them on the prepared baking sheet. Brush them with milk or single cream, sprinkle on the rest of the cheese and bake for about 15–18 minutes, until golden on top.

TIPS
- Sage works well as an alternative to chives.
- Measuring Marmite can be fiddly. Dip the measuring spoon into boiling water first, or wipe it with a little cooking oil, to make it easier.
- If it's a hot day, or if you're hot, or if the kitchen's hot, any or all of the above, run your hands under the cold tap for a bit before drying them well and then rubbing the butter into the flour.

Chapter 6

~

No one wants brunch

NO ONE, OUTSIDE OF A NORA EPHRON MOVIE, WANTS BRUNCH. What is it, for a start? Who needs to be up, hair brushed, dressed and talking any earlier than they have to, particularly at the weekend when brunch is most likely to be inflicted upon us? No one knows what to wear or – like the time I had that job interview with a famous chef in a yurt – how to sit. Upright at the table? Slummocking on the sofa? I know I may look like I'm wearing an old grey school sweater, but it's clean and it's cashmere, surely that's enough? What more do you want from me?

I experienced my first brunch on 10th November 1991. I know this, not because I have a profoundly accurate memory for mid-morning baskets of brioche, but because I was in New York with a boyfriend, The Correspondent. The previous Wednesday, somewhere off the Canary Islands, shady newspaper mogul Robert Maxwell shadily transitioned from the deck of his yacht, the *Lady Ghislaine* (yes, her), into the water in the middle of the night. Splash. And it certainly was the splash in all the Sunday papers, behind which The Correspondent camouflaged himself. I sat on a mint green velour banquette in the self-consciously shiny dining room of a Upper East Side hotel, heroically, silently, working my way through smoked salmon, cod's roe and scrambled eggs as a pianist in the corner of the room gently plink-plinked his way through songs from the shows. Look at me, living.

Back in London, we had a Jewish friend who in his north London mansion block used to throw an open house once a month on Sunday mornings. He piled his kitchen table with bagels (plain, sesame, poppy seed), tubs of Philadelphia cheese and a big platter of thickly cut smoked salmon. I think there might have been finely sliced red onion, bowls of capers and wedges of lemon too, or I might just be making that up, embellishing the memory for perfection. There were pots of coffee, loads of supermarket champagne, and all the papers. It was lively and loud, and taught me a wonderful thing about generosity and what people really remember. Serve a few things generously. Put your life on big plates. Make it fun.

Having once been a brunch sceptic, I have slowly come around to the idea, though not the 90s performative version of LOOK AT US SPENDING A FORTUNE ON TOAST ON THE LORD'S DAY. I prefer a version of our friend's bagel breakfasts. If you're keen to see your friends but don't want to spend a fortune or put on shoes, inviting people round for brunch might be for you. Just make sure you get the time right (godssake don't expect people to be upright and hammering out their best anecdotes before noon). You want something that starts about midday, and then ambles gently through the afternoon.

I like to make something easy which I can prepare ahead, such as a tomatoey base for shakshuka, so I can just crack the eggs in when people arrive before bunging it in the oven, or the eggs Benedict strata, here (page 88). I make big plates of sausages and bacon, or smoked salmon with some good bread and butter, and just let people help themselves. I usually chop up some fruit, and serve a fresh juice of some kind. I find those guests who like a task love to get to work with the electric citrus press and a heap of oranges. I shake up pitchers of cocktails (very easy ones, we've all just got up), add cafetières of coffee and throw a heap of papers in the middle of the room. And that is really it. There may be show tunes, or old vinyl, depending on the crowd. We might end up watching a favourite movie. It's a lot less work than lunch, and everyone's home, face washed, homework done, at a civilized hour, ready to submit once more to the tyranny of the week, full of friendship and bagels.

Eggs Benedict strata

SERVES ~ 6–8

Like all sane people, I love eggs Benedict. But I seldom want to make eggs
Benedict, particularly for a crowd, particularly in the morning, which is exactly
when you normally want eggs Benedict. So I came up with this recipe, which is a
strata – a sort of savoury bread-and-butter pudding – which has all the delicious
qualities of eggs Benedict without the perilous activity of attempting hollandaise
sauce with a hangover. As an added benefit, it's even better if you prepare it the
day before and then just put it into the oven while you're pottering about in your
nightie, waking up, drinking Berocca, making coffee. I add spinach here, to make
a sort of Benedict/Florentine hybrid, but you can leave the spinach out if you
want. It is enough as it is, but rashers of crisp bacon and beautiful sausages are
irresistible, to me at least.

*a little softened butter, for greasing
the dish*

*6–8 white muffins, about 500–600g,
slightly stale (if not stale, see
instructions for stale-ing in the
recipe)*

*a couple of handfuls of baby spinach,
about 70g*

*4 thick slices of ham, about 250g,
roughly torn into approximately
3cm pieces*

120g Gruyère cheese, grated

FOR THE 'HOLLANDAISE'
CUSTARD

160ml white wine vinegar

1 small shallot, diced, about 20g

1 teaspoon black peppercorns

1 bay leaf

8 eggs, lightly beaten

450ml double cream

160ml single cream

a few fine gratings of lemon zest

2 tablespoons lemon juice

3 tablespoons Dijon mustard

salt and freshly ground black pepper

First, make the custard. Put the vinegar into a small pan with the shallot, peppercorns
and bay leaf, and simmer until the vinegar is reduced to about 4 tablespoons. Let it
cool. Whisk together the eggs and creams, strain in the cooled vinegar and gently
stir it all together. Grate over a little lemon zest, being careful not to add any bitter
white pith, then stir in the lemon juice and mustard. Season with 1 teaspoon each
of salt and pepper.

Lightly butter an ovenproof dish (I use a Pyrex dish, 28 × 28 × 8cm, but any ceramic or enamelware gratin dish of approximately those dimensions will do). Split the muffins and roughly tear each piece into quarters. If they aren't stale, toss the torn bread on to a baking sheet and bake it at 160°C/140°C fan/gas 3 for 10 minutes, then remove it from the oven and leave it to cool completely.

Put the pieces of muffin, spinach and ham into the oven dish and mix it all together (with your beautifully clean hands, ideally) so everything is evenly distributed. Slowly add the egg mixture, pouring it evenly over the strata, gently tilting the dish to make sure it reaches every corner. Gently press with the back of a spoon. Cover with foil (you need to cook it under foil for a bit later, so better to use it now than to waste cling film), and refrigerate for at least 4 hours, or ideally overnight.

Remove the strata from the fridge 30 minutes before you want to bake it and spoon over any of the egg mixture that hasn't soaked into the bread. Put the dish on a baking sheet to catch any drips. Preheat the oven to 180°C/160°C fan/gas 4.

Scatter over the cheese. If you didn't cover the strata with foil before, do it now. Bake it for 30 minutes, then remove the foil and continue to cook it for a further 20–30 minutes, until the top has crisped up a little and is turning golden. Let it cool for 5–10 minutes before serving.

VARIATION

You can also add some halved cherry tomatoes to the mixture, if you're some kind of health freak.

Russian breakfast cheesecake

SERVES ~ 6–8

I call this Russian breakfast cheesecake because when I lived in Moscow it was the sort of thing served in the few smart hotels as part of their breakfast buffets, along with the pancakes, sour cream, caviar, smoked fish and cured meats. The most spectacular of these was the Metropol Hotel, with its stained-glass dome and marble fountain – a little pre-Revolutionary decadence with your brunch, madam?

I found a version of breakfast cheesecake in the wonderful book *The Food and Cooking of Russia* by Lesley Chamberlain and cooked it again and again while I was there, tweaking it and adapting it until it evolved into this version here. It's great either on its own or with some fruit – any stone fruit (see nectarines with raspberries and mint, page 93) or figs go with it particularly well.

½ teaspoon finely grated zest from an unwaxed orange – grate it directly on to the curd cheese so as not to lose any of its intense flavour

500g curd cheese (see page 74 if you fancy making your own), or ricotta

juice of 1 large unwaxed orange

40g raisins

40g melted butter, plus a little more for greasing the tin

180g cream cheese

20g caster sugar

20g semolina

1 tablespoon orange flower water

½ teaspoon salt

2 eggs, lightly beaten

120ml sour cream, plus more to serve if you like

This requires a little juggling. It's easier to zest an unsqueezed orange, of course, but you need to squeeze the orange to soak the raisins for a few hours or overnight. I like to zest citrus straight into whatever I am mixing with it – you lose a lot of their delicious oils if you zest them on to a plate as part of your *mise en place* (I know none of us is doing a proper *mise en place*, but let's just pretend for a minute). So when I make this, I zest the orange on to the curd cheese or ricotta, though I don't mix it in until I begin making the cheesecake so the flavour remains delicate and not overwhelmingly orange-y. Then I squeeze the orange juice into a small bowl, add the raisins and leave them to soak.

Chapter 6 ~ No one wants brunch

Generously butter a 23cm springform cake tin and line the base with baking parchment; butter the parchment. Preheat the oven to 160°C/140°C fan/gas 3.

In a large bowl, beat the curd cheese or ricotta with the orange zest until smooth, then beat in the cream cheese until everything is well combined. Fold in the melted butter, sugar, semolina, orange flower water and salt, then gently stir in the eggs. Drain the raisins (drink the juice) and fold them into the mixture. Spoon everything into the prepared tin and smooth the top with a spatula. Pour over the sour cream and smooth it into an even layer.

Place the tin on a baking sheet and bake the cheesecake for 35–40 minutes, until it's set but still has a little wobble in the middle. It should be slightly pulling away from the sides of the tin and turning very lightly golden on top. It will set more as it cools. Let it sit in the tin for 15 minutes before gently loosening the springform catch and sliding it on to a plate, carefully removing the baking parchment as you go. Serve it warm or cold, on its own or with some more sour cream on the side, or with fruit.

~

Nectarines with raspberries and mint

SERVES ˜ 4–8

If they're slipping out of their skins with delight at the height of their season, the nectarines may not need sugar, so taste them before adding it. Or use a trickle of honey instead if you like. Serve this fruit salad either with the breakfast cheesecake (page 91) or with thick Greek yoghurt.

6 ripe nectarines, or a mixture of nectarines and peaches

*1–2 teaspoons caster sugar or vanilla sugar (see **TIP**, page 182), depending on the sweetness of the fruit*

1–2 teaspoons rose water or orange flower water

150g raspberries, or a mixture of raspberries and blueberries

8–10 mint leaves, shredded, plus a few small leaves to finish

25g pistachios, roughly chopped

Halve the nectarines and remove the stones. Slice them thinly, lay them on a plate and scatter over the sugar, then sprinkle on the flower water. Leave for 15 minutes, then, just before serving, gently combine with the raspberries and mint and scatter over the pistachios and small mint leaves.

TIP **HOW TO HALVE A NECTARINE**
Hold the nectarine in the palm of your hand and – staring at the stem end – use a small, sharp knife to cut all the way to the stone and then work your way round, cutting to the stone as you go, until you are back where you started. Twist the fruit and one half will come away. Use your fingernail or the knife to remove the stone from the other half. If the fruit is ripe, this is the work of seconds. If it's not, just do the best you can.

~

Greyhound cocktail

The most important thing about entertaining at the weekend, or at any time, is that it should be as easy as you can possibly make it. Unless you go at cocktail making like some go at an Ironman challenge, or competitive jigsawing, which is to say with great energy, patience and finesse, I advise keeping it simple. I'm muddled enough on a Sunday morning without having to bother with mint and ice cubes. I have a few standby cocktails which I can make by the jug (see world-beating Bloody Mary, page 126), which gives plenty of time for reading the papers and general slummocking about.

I am giving you proportions here, rather than a strict recipe, as it rather depends on how big your jug and your thirst are, and how many people you are serving. Squeezing your own grapefruit juice makes all the difference. I have a simple Braun electric citrus press which cost only about twenty-five pounds and makes creating citrus cocktails a cinch – also very useful for making lemon meringue pies, marmalade and fruit curds. It certainly earns its place on the shelf. Use yellow grapefruit if you prefer, but I like the slightly sweeter hit of pink grapefruit.

1 part vodka

3 parts pink grapefruit juice

lots of ice

wedges of lime and/or slices of pink grapefruit

sparkling water or soda water (optional)

Mix together the vodka and grapefruit juice in a large, chilled jug and stir. Fill some tall glasses with ice, add the sliced fruit and pour over the grapefruit juice and vodka. Top up with sparkling water or soda water for a lighter drink.

ALTERNATIVE

To turn a greyhound into a salty dog, add a salted rim to the glass in the manner of a margarita.

~

Chapter 7

Why everyone hates picnics

EVERY CAR JOURNEY, EVERY SUMMER, MY HUSBAND AND I HAVE THE SAME ARGUMENT: sun roof open or sun roof closed? I am firmly sun roof closed. I like a sunny day as much as the next pale-skinned Anglo-Saxon Factor-50-smothered person with an aversion to her hair whipping about and sticking to her lipstick – all of which is to say, I like the idea probably more than I like the reality. There is an enormous pressure that comes with a warm day, and that is – on our damp little island – the crushing responsibility to enjoy it.

I am enormously keen on comfort. Like a cat, I seek out the softest chairs and the sunniest window seats. I dislike intensely any notion of being 'improved', which is why all forms of exercise that don't serve another purpose – such as walking the dogs or wrestling a herbaceous border into shape – are my idea of hell. My exceptionally vigorous and delightful sister-in-law once tried to jolly me along during a fifteen-minute walk around Buttermere lake in the rain and it was the longest year of my life.

Which is why, when it comes to picnics, I am torn. I quite like the idea of it, but not the intense planning, packing and schlepping that make me feel as relaxed as Lady Hester Stanhope trailing through Lebanon on a donkey, circa 1830. I have put in enough hours heaving wicker hampers through parks, to concerts and plays, along riverbanks, to know that that is quite enough of that, thank you.

But sometimes, you can't avoid it. You are forced to abandon the deep, deep peace of the dining table and fat-bottomed chairs for the hurly-burly of having your tea outside. Are you having fun yet?

My most memorable picnics have been the simplest. Egg sandwiches on the beach in Ireland (page 267), a pork pie eaten sitting on a prickly hay bale at a county show, a 9 a.m. train picnic with food writer friends which comprised an icy thermos of martinis, a bowl of olives and some charcuterie. Fancy.

My most recent picnic of joy was on Christmas morning 2020, when Séan and I were on our own during lockdown in France, the first Christmas we'd ever spent without a house full of people and a fridge full of food. We were woken by the bells ringing out from the Église Saint Jean-Baptiste in the village and the clanking chorus of the rigging on the boats in the harbour. We took the dogs to walk by the water at Marseillan Plage in the chilly pink light of the early morning, only a few other dog walkers around. '*Joyeux Noël*', '*Joyeux Noël*', throw a stick, throw a ball. We had a small bag with a bottle of champagne, a carton of orange juice, a thermos of coffee and wedges of chard frittata wrapped in foil. We threw a hammam towel over a driftwood log and called it a table. That was enough. It was perfect.

So what I am saying to you is you can have a perfectly acceptable picnic – a joyful picnic even – without resorting to footmen and samovars. I often think of this when I watch *Below Deck*, when the crew is tasked with hauling uncomfortable-looking furniture and a full dinner service halfway up a mountain or along the windiest beach so that people who have spent $250,000 to enjoy three days on a superyacht can look at the yacht from a slightly different angle. Inevitably, someone has forgotten the tequila or the caviar and everything is ruined. My life advice is to stay on your superyacht, whatever that looks like to you.

If you must venture out, take with you the very best non-attention-seeking, no-cutlery-requiring food you can muster. Things which come in their own edible wrapping, such as pies, pasties and sausage rolls, are, of course, excellent. Wedges of frittata scrabbled together from what you have in the fridge, spicy chicken wings, and other things you can eat solely with the assistance of squares of kitchen paper hastily torn from the roll, are also highly suitable. I include radishes with anchovy butter here because sometimes you want a little crunch to balance out the pastry, but that could just as easily come from a few pieces of perfect fruit. Add to that a thermos of coffee, a bottle of wine, some beer and/or water and you have quite enough to sustain you until your next meal, which will ideally be inside, once your fresh-air-freak phase has been sated for another year.

Anchovy butter and radishes

SERVES ~ **2–4, depending on what else you have packed**

I am a huge fan of savoury butters of all kinds as a way of injecting instant flavour. I make anchovy butter a lot, but on this occasion I had half a tin of tuna left over and was anxious to use it up (see northern, *passim*), so here we are. Make sure the butter is soft and the radishes super fresh.

a bunch of radishes, well washed (see **TIP** *below), and with the leaves still on for preference and beauty*

FOR THE ANCHOVY BUTTER

100g softened butter

60g tuna in oil, drained

4–5 anchovies in oil, drained

a generous squeeze of lemon

a pinch of seaweed flakes, if you have them, but don't buy them specially

I use my beloved mini food processor to make the anchovy butter, as there isn't enough to process properly in a large one. You could also use a stick blender to make it, or a pestle and mortar. Simply process or pound all the ingredients together until very smooth and well combined. Taste and add more lemon if necessary. Scrape the butter into a bowl, or a plastic container or jam jar if you are taking it on a picnic, with the radishes in a separate container, and sprinkle more seaweed flakes over the top if you want.

VARIATION
Add some stoned black or green olives to the butter before processing.

TIP **HOW TO WASH RADISHES**
You want the beauty of the whole radish, whether they are mild, elegant French breakfast radishes, pleasing little cannonballs, Cherry Belle or Stela, or one of the smart multicoloured varieties you find now in the more recherché greengrocers. The sprightliness of the leaves is the best indicator of how fresh they are, so try always to buy them with the leaves on. Even when they look quite clean, they can be holding on to a lot of grit, which is precisely the crunch you don't want. Fill a bowl with cold water and let them soak for 5 minutes or so – you want them completely submerged, leaves and all. Drain

and repeat, rubbing off any surface dirt you can see, until there is no grit left in the bowl. Lay them on a clean tea towel to dry, and eat as soon as you can. If you are preparing them for a party, you can simply roll them up in the damp tea towel and keep them in the fridge for up to four or five hours.

~

Sticky honey chicken wings

SERVES ~ **8–10**

Between you and me, I could probably eat all these on my own. This should go no further, you understand.

8–10 chicken wings, about 1kg

FOR THE MARINADE
150ml runny honey

100ml dark soy sauce

4 cloves of garlic, halved, green germ removed, and very finely chopped

1 tablespoon Tabasco sauce

1 tablespoon concentrated tomato purée

1 tablespoon ground ginger

FOR THE COOL HERB DIP
200ml sour cream

80ml mayonnaise

2 cloves of garlic, halved, green germ removed, and very finely chopped

3 tablespoons chopped fresh chives

3 tablespoons chopped fresh parsley leaves

2 tablespoons chopped fresh dill

½ teaspoon English mustard powder

salt and freshly ground black pepper

In a large bowl, whisk together everything for the marinade and add the chicken wings. Turn them over and make sure they are very well coated, then cover and refrigerate for at least 4 hours, or overnight. Take them out of the fridge about an hour before you want to cook them.

Preheat the oven to 200°C/180°C fan/gas 6. Line a large baking tray with foil and arrange the wings on it, leaving space between them. Pour over any extra marinade and roast for 40–45 minutes, turning once or twice.

In a bowl, whisk together all the ingredients for the dip and serve it alongside the wings, with lots of paper napkins.

TIP
You can also cook these on the barbecue if you want. Place them on a medium–hot part of the barbecue and cook for about 20–25 minutes, turning periodically and brushing with the marinade a couple of times – you should let them cook for at least 10 minutes after the final brush of marinade.

~

Sausage rolls three ways

SERVES ~ 8–12

Is there a better friend to a picnic than a sausage roll? They come in their own handy packaging and you can fill them with all manner of things. If you use bought puff pastry, they're very quick to make too. I give you the method and three of my favourite fillings here, but I hope you'll feel free to create your own. Like frittate (see page III), they're a brilliant way to use up leftovers.

1 × 320g sheet of ready-rolled all-butter puff pastry (these are usually about 23 × 35cm)

1 egg, lightly beaten with 1 tablespoon water

Unroll the pastry but keep it on the paper or plastic sheet it comes on and place it on a baking tray lined with non-stick baking parchment or Silpat. Cut the pastry in half lengthways.

Prepare the filling, as described in the recipes below.

Brush the edge of the pastry furthest away from you with egg wash and arrange half the filling along the length of the pastry. It should be slightly off centre, and slightly closer to you. Use the paper or plastic sheet to help you roll the pastry over, tucking it in with your fingers as you go, on to the egg-washed edge, pressing to seal. Turn the baking sheet around and repeat with the other half of the pastry. Put them in the fridge to chill for 30 minutes.

Preheat the oven to 220°C/200°C fan/gas 7.

Cut each roll into 4–6 pieces (4 is more great outdoors, 6 is more drinks party). Remove the sheet of paper or plastic you used to help you roll them up, and arrange the sausage rolls on the prepared tray, seam side down. Brush them with the egg wash and season as described in the recipe. Bake for 20 minutes, until the filling is piping hot and the pastry is golden.

Potato, Cheddar and spring onion rolls

250g cooked potato, cut into small dice

120g Cheddar cheese, grated, plus a further 20g to scatter over the top

3 spring onions, trimmed and finely chopped, about 30g

3 tablespoons crème fraîche

2 tablespoons finely chopped fresh parsley leaves

½ teaspoon freshly ground black pepper, plus a few grinds for the top of the rolls

½ teaspoon caraway seeds, plus more for sprinkling on top

Mix everything together gently with a spatula, until well combined. Add salt to taste – this will vary depending on how salty your Cheddar is. After you brush the sausage rolls with the egg wash, scatter on some caraway seeds and grated cheese, along with a few grinds of pepper.

Toulouse sausage rolls

Of course, you can just use Toulouse sausages from the butcher – or any favourite sausages – removed from their casings to fill your sausage rolls, but it is quite fun to make your own filling too.

500g minced pork, quite coarsely minced if possible, but don't get too hung up on it

50ml red wine

2 tablespoons garlic powder, or 4 cloves of fresh garlic, halved, green germ removed, and very finely chopped

1½ tablespoons freshly ground black pepper

2 teaspoons salt

½ teaspoon herbes de Provence or dried thyme

¼ teaspoon freshly grated nutmeg

freshly ground black pepper

1 tablespoon Dijon mustard

Mix together all the ingredients apart from the mustard. Use your hands and get right in there, making sure they are very well combined. Cover and leave overnight in the fridge for the flavours to develop.

When you open out the pastry and halve it lengthways, brush the mustard on to the pastry, leaving a 1cm border all around, before you add the meat. After you brush the tops of the rolls with the egg wash, grind on some black pepper before they go into the oven.

~

Koulibiac rolls

I love these, a slightly retro treat inspired by the Russian classic of salmon, rice and eggs encased in pastry.

a knob of unsalted butter, about 20g

1 torpedo shallot, about 70g, finely diced

salt and freshly ground black pepper

1 salmon fillet, about 220g, poached, skin removed

100g cooked basmati rice

2 hard-boiled eggs, roughly chopped

2 tablespoons fresh dill fronds, chopped

finely grated zest of ½ an unwaxed lemon (grate it directly into the bowl with the rice and fish)

1 tablespoon lemon juice

flaky sea salt

Melt the butter over a medium–low heat in a small frying pan and sauté the shallot with a pinch of salt until just softened, about 5 minutes. Tip it into a bowl to cool. Break the salmon up into large-ish flakes and add it to the shallot, along with the rice, eggs, dill, lemon zest and juice, and ½ teaspoon each of salt and freshly ground black pepper. Turn it over gently with a spatula until just combined.

After you brush the tops of the koulibiac rolls with the egg wash, sprinkle on a little flaky sea salt before putting them into the oven.

~

Frittate forever

Robust frittate make excellent picnic food, or packed lunch food, or 'What shall I do with all these leftovers?' food. I make them all the time and no two are ever the same, as it so depends on my mood and what's in the fridge as to what goes into them, but these three – or versions of them with slight tweaks – are in frequent rotation in my kitchen.

Asparagus, new potatoes and peas

50g crème fraîche

8 eggs, lightly beaten

50g Parmesan cheese, finely grated

3 tablespoons chopped fresh parsley leaves

2 teaspoons chopped fresh tarragon or chervil leaves

salt and freshly ground black pepper

250g new potatoes, cooked in their skins, then peeled and quartered

200g cooked thin asparagus, cut into 5cm pieces, tips separated from the rest

100g peas, cooked

40g unsalted butter

150g ricotta

Preheat the oven to 190°C/170°C fan/gas 5.

Put the crème fraîche into the bottom of a large bowl, add about a quarter of the egg and whisk with a fork until well combined. Add the rest of the eggs. Whisk in half the Parmesan and all the herbs, and season very well with salt and pepper.

Add the potatoes, the asparagus apart from the tips – put them to one side for now – and the peas. Give it all a good stir.

In a heavy-bottomed non-stick frying pan, approximately 25–30cm diameter, melt the butter over a medium heat. Swirl it around so the surface of the pan is coated. Tip in the frittata mixture and smooth the ingredients out so they're evenly spread across the pan. Arrange the asparagus tips over the top of the frittata, dot on the ricotta and sprinkle on the remaining Parmesan. Let the eggs cook gently for about 5 minutes, setting from the bottom up. Then put the pan into the oven – if the handle isn't ovenproof, wrap it in a couple of tight layers of aluminium foil to protect it – and cook for around 12 minutes, until just set and golden on top.

Remove the pan from the oven and let the frittata set and cool for 10 minutes, until it pulls away from the edges slightly, before cutting. Eat warm or cold.

Bacon, red pepper and feta frittata

4 tablespoons olive oil

180g streaky bacon, smoked or unsmoked, cut into 1cm pieces

1 red pepper, about 120g, halved, deseeded and diced

1 red onion, about 120g, diced

2 cloves of garlic, halved, green germ removed, diced

50g crème fraîche

8 eggs, lightly beaten

4 tablespoons roughly chopped fresh parsley leaves

2 tablespoons roughly chopped fresh dill

a good pinch of chilli flakes

salt and freshly ground black pepper

200g feta, cut into 1cm cubes

50g stoned, chopped green olives

3 spring onions, trimmed and finely sliced

In a heavy-bottomed non-stick frying pan, approximately 25–30cm diameter, warm 3 tablespoons of the oil over a medium–high heat. Add the bacon and sauté it, stirring from time to time, until it's golden and has rendered its fat, about 5–7 minutes. Reduce the temperature a little, add the red pepper and onion and fry for 5 minutes until softened. Add the garlic and fry gently for a minute. Remove the pan from the heat and let everything cool for 10 minutes.

Preheat the oven to 190°C/170°C fan/gas 5.

Put the crème fraîche into a large bowl, add about a quarter of the egg and whisk with a fork until well combined. Add the rest of the eggs. Whisk in the herbs and chilli flakes, and season very well with salt and pepper – I add ½ teaspoon of salt and ½ teaspoon of pepper, but it depends a little on how salty the bacon is. Fold in the feta, olives and spring onions, then tip in the cooled bacon, pepper and onion and give everything a good stir.

Put the frying pan back on the hob, over a medium heat, and warm the remaining tablespoon of oil, swirling it round the pan. Pour in the frittata mixture and smooth the ingredients out so they're evenly spread across the pan. Let the eggs cook gently for about 5 minutes, setting from the bottom up. Then put the pan into the oven – if the handle isn't ovenproof, wrap it in a couple of tight layers of aluminium foil to protect it – and cook for around 12 minutes, until just set and golden on top.

Remove the pan from the oven and let the frittata set and cool for 10 minutes, until it pulls away from the edges slightly, before cutting. Eat warm or cold.

~

Smoked mackerel and spinach with horseradish cream

60g unsalted butter

50g baby spinach, washed, with the rinsing water still clinging to the leaves

1 smoked mackerel fillet, about 220g

3 spring onions, about 30g, trimmed and finely chopped

4 tablespoons chopped fresh parsley leaves

3 tablespoons chopped fresh dill fronds

8 eggs, lightly beaten

salt and freshly ground black pepper

3 tablespoons crème fraîche

1 tablespoon horseradish sauce

Preheat the oven to 190°C/170°C fan/gas 5.

In a heavy-bottomed non-stick frying pan, approximately 25–30cm diameter, melt 20g of the butter over a medium heat. Add the spinach, stir, and put the lid on for a minute or two until the leaves are just wilted. Tip into a colander and let it cool. Wipe the pan out with a piece of kitchen paper and put it back on the stove.

Put the spinach into a bowl. Break the mackerel into pieces, discarding the skin, and put it into the bowl with the spinach. Add the spring onions and herbs, pour in the eggs and stir until well combined. Season with salt and pepper – bear in mind that the mackerel is quite salty.

Melt the remaining butter in the pan over a medium heat and swirl it around so the surface of the pan is coated. Tip in the frittata mixture and smooth the ingredients out so they're evenly spread across the pan. Let the eggs cook gently for about 5 minutes, setting from the bottom up. While they're cooking, whisk together the crème fraîche and horseradish. Dot the horseradish cream over the top of the frittata, then put the pan into the oven – if the handle isn't ovenproof, wrap it in a couple of tight layers of aluminium foil to protect it – and cook for around 12 minutes, until just set and golden on top.

Remove the pan from the oven and let the frittata set and cool for 10 minutes, until it pulls away from the edges slightly, before cutting. Eat warm or cold.

~

Chapter 8

How to survive having people to stay

IT COMES TO US ALL IN THE END. You blithely run about your life shouting, 'You must come and stay for the weekend!' as you jump into taxis, then, particularly if you live in an exciting city, or by the sea, or in a beautiful part of the countryside, eventually people will take you up on it. By the time you get to setting up a Doodle planner, it's too late to wriggle out.

And honestly, you shouldn't. To paraphrase Granny, you'll enjoy it when they get here. Probably.

Having your best belovèds to stay for the weekend can be about as restful as putting on tights in a roomful of kittens. But with some preparation, you can minimize risks of exhaustion and maximize the possibility of getting to Sunday with your relationships and your sanity intact. This is the place where I'm supposed to say, in lifestyle-magazine-speak, that it's so easy, all you need is a willing heart, an icy bottle of vodka and a hula hoop, or some such nonsense. The truth is the preparation is hard work, but if you do as much as possible ahead, you get to enjoy the weekend too – and its aftermath: a superlatively clean house, some fluffy new towels which haven't been used to bath the dog, and potentially a fridge full of cheese – so everybody wins.

The best way to survive the rolling, all-you-can-eat buffet that is having visitors to stay is to invite only people you really like, never people you want to impress or show off to (see always-right Lola, page 52). And make it very clear when you would like them to arrive, say, in time for drinks on Friday, and, MOST IMPORTANTLY, when you expect them to leave, possibly after lunch on Sunday.

The other torturing piece of ambiguity for guests and hosts is knowing what you are allowed to eat. I hate that gnawing feeling of being stuck in someone else's house with no possibility of a midnight sandwich. Because then all I want is a midnight sandwich. When Séan and I were on our honeymoon in Ireland, we stayed at Delphi Lodge, a beautiful nineteenth-century fishing lodge in Connemara. Back then it was an exquisitely simple place, without the swags-and-tails obvious luxe it's acquired in recent years. It was just a big, beautiful house with a tomato-red door, the mountains behind and the loch in front. We arrived late in the afternoon, hoping we'd found the right place, as there were no signs on the road to indicate it was a hotel (Prince Charles had stayed there a couple of years previously, and I think the absence of signs had been an attempt to deter gawpers). We knocked and no one came. We let ourselves into the hushed hall. Just as we were wondering if we were perhaps committing a very genteel act of breaking and entering, a young woman dashed down the stairs. 'HALLOOO, you must be the Donnellans. Shall I take you to your room now, or would you like to sit in the library with some tea? Chef's just made a lovely chocolate cake. We don't have room service as such, but if you're hungry just help yourselves from the kitchen. Try not to eat anything that's too obviously tonight's dinner!'

To this day, I begin visits to our house by telling guests to help themselves to anything, but just to try not to eat anything that's too obviously tonight's dinner. You have to make it easy for people. We once had a friend staying in our house while we were away. He called me to say there was absolutely nothing to eat (I love him, he's like my annoying little brother, it's fine, hello Richard). This puzzled me, as I keep a full larder and fridge at all times. What he meant was, there was nothing to eat RIGHT NOW

THIS MINUTE. It was all ingredients. So now, I always make sure the fridge is full of obvious snacks: olives, salamis, pots of hummus and crudités, an abundance of cheese, antipasti plundered from the chiller cabinet at Gallo Nero on the High Street. And of course there must always be bread and crackers and an abundance of crisps of all kinds. Set out a drinks table or tray too, with glasses, spirits, ice buckets, chopping boards and knives waiting for fruit and other garnishes, so that you are never more than seconds away from cocktail hour. Keeping this fresh and stocked is a good job to delegate to someone else. It will help them feel included in ensuring the jollity of the masses and it's one less thing for you to do.

It is quite spoilingly kind to leave treats for your guests in their rooms, such as a bowl of beautiful fruit, a tin of favourite biscuits and some really good chocolate. I've always been in two minds about the B&B-style tea tray. On the one hand, it feels naff. On the other, it's nice for your guests to be able to make themselves a cup of tea in the middle of the night without crashing around and waking everyone up looking for the non-existent artificial sweeteners.

When it comes to feeding the hordes, don't do everything from scratch (see How to throw a party without losing your mind, page 50) and plan to eat out at least once during the course of the weekend. This isn't just to give you a break; it is good for everyone to get out of the house, so you don't become like some hermetically sealed Scandi-noir drama of barely concealed angst.

Plan the meals you are going to eat at home, and try to include something special in each one. It doesn't need to be complicated. In fact, it shouldn't be. We all have enough on. Poaching quince (page 122) and making your own granola (page 125) are simple enough – and you can do lots, so you have plenty left over when your guests leave – but elevate the simplest of breakfasts. Gruyère and anchovy puffs (page 128) are an easy-but-still-fancy alternative to gougères to go with drinks. Roasting a whole fish instead of a piece of meat looks impressive, but is a little lighter during a weekend of bacchanalian excess. The components for a berry crostata (page 133) can all be prepared ahead, then assembled in minutes and baked just before you want to eat it, filling the whole house with gold-star Domestic Goddess aromas.

As the late Antonio Carluccio used to say, 'MOF MOF! Minimum of fuss, maximum of flavour.'

All these party principles can be scaled up or down, depending on whether you have two people or ten, on how much time you have at your disposal, and how gleefully you embrace the prep. Don't bite off more than you can happily chew; you risk ending up a resentful, exhausted mess. Your friends are here to see you and enjoy your company, and too much huffing and puffing and bossing about from you will make them feel like a burden. They probably experience enough of that in their day jobs – no one needs it in their playtime too, not least you. Balance buying in, eating out, plating up, and let the good times roll.

~

Creating a beautiful no-cook platter

- Sometimes snacks are as good as dinner, particularly if you're all a little overexcited at being together. You won't want to do this for every meal, but sometimes – lunch in the garden, for example, or in the evening in front of the fire – it can be really delightful, particularly if during the rest of the weekend you've planned a lot of sit-down feasts.

- First, take your largest platter, or several platters, or wooden boards. When I'm doing this for a big crowd, I spread it all out along a slate column which once must have supported a fireplace mantel in our house. I found it in the cellar one day, gave it a good scrub and it has played host to cheese and salamis of many nations ever since.

- Don't smoosh everything together. Give different components space to breathe.

- Everything needs to be small enough to be consumed in one or two bites.

- Choose two or three different cheeses which are easy to handle (blue cheese can be a bit crumbly), and two or three different types of cured meat – I like Parma ham gently folded on to the board like petals, finocchiona, the Tuscan salami seasoned warmly with fennel, and chorizo or jamón ibérico.

- Add small bowls of olives and cornichons.

- Dips are a good chance to add colour, so instead of just plonking down a bowl of hummus, think about ones based on roasted peppers, squash, avocado or beetroot.

- Add colourful, crunchy vegetables. Whole radishes and the conveniently scoop-shaped leaves of endive look wonderful.

- Arrange some fresh and dried fruit on the platter – grapes, cut figs, dried apricots and prunes are good. Scatter on some nuts too – pistachios in their shells and Marcona almonds are perfect.

- Place one or two different kinds of crackers, and possibly some breadsticks, in among the rest of the bounty.

- Make sure you add toothpicks if required and small bowls for olive stones and other debris. There is no shame in using paper napkins with this either – get some pretty, cocktail-sized ones. I am slightly obsessed with these and collect them on my travels.

~

How to assemble an afternoon tea

- If you can't cram in an extra opportunity for a meal when you have friends to stay, when can you? Keep things fairly simple and small, as you don't want it to get in the way of eating dinner later.

- Simple sandwiches, fairly thinly filled. Cut the crusts off if you like, or don't. I like cucumber sandwiches on white bread, ham sandwiches on brown bread with a whack of English mustard, tiny rolls filled with egg salad. This isn't the time to reinvent the sandwich.

- Scones, of course. Lemon and buttermilk scones (page 79) and Cheddar and Marmite scones (page 81) are both very good, but as with all things, if you are lucky enough to have a great baker nearby, there is no shame at all in buying them. My only word of caution is that bought scones are often enormous; do try to hunt down small ones if you can.

- You will need a cake. I like a fairly simple one such as the burnt honey and walnut cake (page 186) or the plum cake (page 181).

- I know champagne teas are all the rage now, but I really like to drink tea with my tea. Beautiful loose-leaf tea made in a teapot and served in bone china cups is made to go with this kind of food, whereas I think champagne gets lost in all the sugar. Save it for before or afterwards, but drink tea during is my advice to you, which you can do with as you will.

Poached quince with rosemary and honey

SERVES ~ 4–6

I like to use sprigs of ginger rosemary for this, from a plant given to me by my friend Mark Diacono of Otter Farm, but any rosemary will do. This makes a wonderful breakfast with Greek yoghurt but – more indulgently – is a tarte Tatin in waiting. I highly recommend using quince in place of apples sometimes, in the recipe on page 201.

2–3 sprigs of rosemary

a strip of zest from an unwaxed orange, pared off with a sharp vegetable peeler, white pith removed

4 quince, about 1kg, peeled, quartered and cored

200ml sweet white or red wine

juice of 1 orange

juice of ½ a lemon

50g runny honey

50g butter

TO SERVE

Greek yoghurt, granola (see page 125)

Preheat the oven to 180°C/160°C fan/gas 4.

Lay the rosemary sprigs and orange zest in the bottom of a roasting tin and place the quince, cut side up, on top. Pour over the wine, orange and lemon juice and trickle on the honey. Place a scrap of butter on each quince. Cover the tin tightly with foil (you could also make a foil packet to contain the quince, which will make it easier to clean the tin, as with cooking beetroot on page 221). Bake for 1 hour. Remove the foil, baste with the juices, then return, uncovered, to the oven and continue to bake until tender when pierced with a small, sharp knife – about 45 minutes, though it could easily take longer. They're a quirky fruit. I have had them take up to an hour and a half longer – just remember to baste them every 20 minutes or so. They'll get there. It's not you, it's them.

Serve with yoghurt, and/or granola for health, with the syrup trickled over the top. If you have an excess of syrup, it's delicious in cocktails – try it with gin or vodka over ice, topped up with tonic.

~

Granola for health

MAKES ~ about 10 servings when eaten as cereal, about 20 servings when used to top yoghurt

I am generally averse to breakfast cereal, because mornings can be quite challenging enough without having to chomp through something where every bite is the same. (I have similar feelings towards some soups and some risottos.) I make an exception for granola, though, as if you do it right, each spoonful can be different from the next. Do use this recipe as a template for your own – add different nuts, seeds and dried fruits, until you create a blend you like. Serve it simply with milk, or layer it up with yoghurt and fresh fruit into 'breakfast trifle'. (Obviously the best breakfast trifle is proper trifle, left over from the night before.)

350g rolled jumbo oats

170g pumpkin seeds

150g pecans, roughly chopped

100g flaked almonds

½ teaspoon flaky sea salt (optional)

¼ teaspoon ground cardamom

¼ teaspoon ground cinnamon – feel free to add more, I just prefer it as a subtle back note

4 tablespoons sunflower oil

100ml maple syrup

40ml runny honey

180g dried cherries

150g dried apricots, chopped

finely grated zest of 1 unwaxed orange (optional) – grate it directly on to the granola

Preheat the oven to 160°C/140°C fan/ gas 3. Line a large baking tray with non-stick baking parchment or Silpat – I use a tray that's 43 × 31 × 2.5cm, and if yours is smaller, the granola might just take slightly longer to cook, or you might want to use two trays.

In a large bowl, mix together the oats, pumpkin seeds, pecans, almonds, salt (if using) and spices. In a small saucepan, gently warm the sunflower oil with the maple syrup and honey, stirring until just combined. Pour it over the oat mixture and stir until everything is really well coated. Spread the granola out on the baking sheet and bake for 35–40 minutes, turning every 10 minutes so it cooks evenly. You want it to be just golden and toasted – don't let it get too dark. Remove the tray from the oven, immediately stir in the dried fruit (and the orange zest, if using), and leave everything to cool together completely on the tray. It will crisp up as it cools. When it's cold, seal in an airtight container, where it will keep for up to a month.

~

How to make a world-beating Bloody Mary

SERVES ~ 1

In the 1952 edition of his book *The Fine Art of Mixing Drinks*, David Embury wrote that the Bloody Mary was a 'classic example of combining in one potion both the poison and the antidote'. This was also the first cocktail guide to include a splash of Tabasco sauce, for that soul-reviving sting of heat.

Whether a Bloody Mary is a meal or a drink has become blurred in recent years. Certainly in my part of East London you are quite likely to find a skewer with bacon or shrimp balanced clumsily on the top of your glass. Personally, I like to let a drink be a drink, with the only adornment being a slim stick of celery, which is more stirrer than nourishment.

I give the measures here for a single drink, but it can easily be made up into a pitcher. In fact, if I'm making these for a restorative brunch or Sunday lunch, I often make up the seasoned tomato juice the night before and refrigerate it, then just add the booze the next day.

A Bloody Mary is a very personal thing. You may or may not want to add horseradish sauce or sherry, you might want more or less Tabasco. It's worth spending an afternoon perfecting your personal technique is all I'm saying. It's an essential life skill, just as much as knowing how to sew on a button or plant a tree.

ice	*½ teaspoon horseradish sauce*
1 part vodka	*a couple of dashes of Tabasco sauce*
2 parts tomato juice	*a dash of Worcestershire sauce*
a good squeeze of lemon or lime juice	*a dash of celery salt*
a splash of dry sherry	*a slim celery stick, for stirring*

I like quite a clean, well-blended drink, so I put a couple of ice cubes into a cocktail shaker, pour over the vodka and tomato juice, lemon or lime juice, add the rest of the ingredients apart from the celery and give it a good shake before straining it into a tall glass with a few big ice cubes in it. Add a celery stick to stir.

~

Gruyère and anchovy puffs

MAKES ~ **about 25, depending on the size of the pastry**

These are so delicious with drinks. Do not deprive yourself.

*2 rectangles of ready-made all-butter
  puff pastry, approximately
  32 × 23cm*

100g Gruyère cheese, grated

*10–12 anchovies in oil, drained and
  roughly chopped*

*1 egg, lightly beaten with
  1 tablespoon water*

FOR THE BÉCHAMEL

20g unsalted butter

1 small shallot, finely diced

1 small bay leaf

20g plain flour

250ml whole milk

50g Gruyère cheese, grated

2 teaspoons Dijon mustard

salt and freshly ground black pepper

First, make the béchamel. In a small saucepan over a medium–low heat, melt the
butter. Add the shallot and the bay leaf and sauté for 5 minutes, stirring now and
then. Add the flour and stir constantly for 3–4 minutes, then remove from the heat
and gradually whisk in the milk until smooth. Return the pan to a medium heat
and stir until the sauce simmers and thickens, about 5 minutes.

Remove the pan from the heat and add the cheese, stirring until it melts,
then stir in the mustard. Taste and season well with salt and pepper. Decant into
a bowl, cool, cover with cling film and chill in the fridge until very cold. You can
do this the day before if you like.

Lay one of the sheets of puff pastry on a chopping board and spread with
the béchamel, all the way to the edges. Scatter on two-thirds of the cheese and all
the anchovies, making sure they're evenly spaced across the pastry. Lay the second
sheet of pastry over the top and press it down lightly.

Chill for 15 minutes in the fridge. If you're making these for a party, you
can prepare them to this stage up to 6 hours ahead.

Heat the oven to 200°C/180°C fan/gas 6. Line a baking sheet with non-stick
baking parchment or Silpat. With a sharp knife, cut the pastry into approximately
4–5cm squares. Place them on the prepared sheet with a little space between them
so they can puff up a bit. Brush with the egg wash and scatter the remaining cheese
over the top. Add a few grinds of black pepper and bake for 12 minutes, until
golden. Serve immediately.

ALTERNATIVE

This is a simple recipe which lends itself to endless adaptations. Try Cheddar with ham, goat's cheese and figs, or chopped black or green olives with crumbled feta.

~

An updated Sunday lunch: whole roast sea bass

SERVES ~ 4–6, depending what else you are serving

A lot of people are intimidated by cooking fish, but it's the first thing they order when they go to a restaurant. It's understandable. It isn't cheap, you can overcook it easily and it usually needs to be cooked at the last minute. But cooking a whole fish takes away those pressures and it looks really wonderful when you bring it out to the table. If you have a crowd, you can easily do two trays – you can also do all the prep a couple of hours in advance and just start cooking about 45 minutes before you want to eat. The fish has a better flavour when it's cooked on the bone too.

80ml extra virgin olive oil, plus a little more to finish – use your good oil

2 strips of lemon zest, about 6cm, carefully pared from an unwaxed lemon with a sharp vegetable peeler, making sure you don't remove any bitter white pith

1 teaspoon fennel seeds, lightly crushed

1kg waxy potatoes, such as Anya or Charlotte

1 small bulb of fennel, about 350–400g

a small bunch of fresh lemon thyme, about 6–7 sprigs

2 torpedo shallots, about 140g, halved and thinly sliced

5 sprigs of fresh tarragon

4 bay leaves

juice of 2 unwaxed lemons

salt and freshly ground black pepper

1 large sea bream or sea bass, about 1kg, scaled and gutted – get the fishmonger to do this for you

TO SERVE
lemon wedges

Put the oil into a small pan with the lemon zest and fennel seeds. Warm gently, without letting it simmer, for 5 minutes, then remove from the heat and cool.

Preheat the oven to 200°C/180°C fan/gas 6.

While the oil is cooling, prepare the vegetables. Peel the potatoes and slice them thinly. If you're a mandolin kind of person, use that. I am not a mandolin kind of person and after a long, bloodstained history of pretending that I am, I hope you won't mind if I just sit quietly over here with a sharp knife and a chopping board and do the best I can to get skinny little slices of potato without having to ruin Sunday lunch by rushing to A&E. I did once go to Sunday lunch at our friends Fred and Kay's, and Fred cut his hand on a tin of foie gras. He ran off to A&E, got himself stitched up and was back before the main course was served,

and despite his admirable sangfroid (and also sang all over the place), it's not ideal. Quarter the fennel, remove the tough core, then slice the quarters thinly (see above). If your fennel has fronds, save some to put inside the roasting fish. Remove the leaves from 4–5 sprigs of the thyme.

Brush a little of the seasoned oil all over the inside of a roasting tin or ceramic gratin dish which is large enough to hold the fish. Put the potatoes, fennel and shallots into the tin with the thyme leaves, 4 sprigs of the tarragon and 3 of the bay leaves, and pour over about 3 tablespoons of the oil (hold back the strip of lemon zest, but let some of the fennel seeds drop in there). Trickle on the lemon juice and season with a teaspoon each of salt and pepper. Give everything a very good stir, then pat it all down into an even layer. Cover it tightly with foil and put it into the oven to roast for about 30–40 minutes, removing it from the oven once to turn everything over before covering it again and returning it to the oven. When all the vegetables are quite tender, remove the foil and whack the oven up to 220°C/200°C fan/gas 7. Make sure it's up to temperature before you put the fish in.

Prepare the fish by cutting 3 or 4 diagonal slashes almost to the bone on both sides. Place the fish on top of the vegetables and brush it all over with the oil, inside the cavity and into the cuts, and all over the skin. Put the strip of lemon zest, the remaining thyme sprigs, tarragon sprig and bay leaf inside the fish, along with some of the fennel seeds and any fennel fronds if you have them. Season the fish with salt and pepper and return the whole tray, uncovered, to the hot hot hot oven. Roast for 20 minutes, until the fish is just cooked through – to test this, press a small, sharp knife into one of the cuts and if you can gently scrape some of the flesh away from the bone without resistance, it's done. Rest for 5 minutes before serving (but make sure the plates are warmed), with a little more of the fruity olive oil trickled over the top.

~

Quick berry crostata

This is the simple tart I make all summer long in France, with berries or peaches or nectarines, or combinations of all of those – whatever I find that looks good in the market or in O' Petit Primeur, our favourite greengrocer's by the church. I confess that when I'm there and it's so hot butter begins melting as you remove it from its wrapper, I'm most likely to make it with bought pastry – you can buy excellent circles of 33cm all-butter pastry in almost every supermarket – so use bought pastry if you want, no one's looking. Or use the recipe here, which you'll need to chill for an hour before using.

This is a wonderful, easy way to end a meal, but do try to save a slice for your breakfast the next morning. It's a heavenly way to start the day, with a trickle of cold cold cream or some crème fraîche.

1 circle of shortcrust all-butter pastry, approximately 33cm diameter

OR

FOR THE PASTRY

160g plain flour or 120g flour and 40g ground almonds, plus more flour for dusting

½ teaspoon salt

80g unsalted butter, very cold, cut into small cubes

80g caster sugar or vanilla sugar (see **TIP**, page 182)

½ teaspoon vanilla extract, if not using vanilla sugar

1 egg, lightly beaten

iced water

FOR THE FILLING

3 tablespoons ground almonds

3 tablespoons caster sugar or vanilla sugar, plus a little more to finish

about 500g berries – I use a combination of raspberries, blueberries and blackcurrants, and sometimes I add blackberries or peaches too, depending on what I have

1 egg, beaten with a splash of water, or some cream

TO SERVE

crème fraîche, vanilla ice cream or cold, thick cream

First, make the pastry. Whisk the ground almonds with the flour if you are combining them, then whisk in the salt. Rub in the butter with your fingers – you still want some pea-sized pieces of butter left in the mixture. Add the sugar and whisk it in with a fork. If you are using vanilla extract, whisk it in with the egg.

Gently cut the egg into the dough a little at a time with a dinner knife until it begins to come together – you may need to add a little iced water, but go gently. Place a sheet of cling film on the counter and turn the dough out on to it, then very gently knead it into a disc. Wrap it up and refrigerate it for at least an hour or up to a day. It is quite a tender dough, and using the cling film like this helps ensure you don't overwork it.

Preheat the oven to 190°C/170°C fan/gas 5. Line a baking sheet with non-stick baking parchment or Silpat. Roll out the pastry into a 30cm-ish circle, between two sheets of cling film or baking parchment lightly dusted with flour. Lay it on the baking sheet and chill it in the fridge for 15 minutes.

Mix the ground almonds with 1 tablespoon of the sugar and scatter it over the pastry – this helps stop the crostata from becoming soggy from the fruit's juices. In a bowl, mix the fruit with the remaining sugar, then heap it on to the pastry, leaving a border of 5cm free of fruit all around the edge. Fold the pastry border back over the fruit – don't worry if it's not perfect, that's part of its raggy, rustic charm – then brush with the egg wash or some cream and sprinkle with a little more sugar. Bake for 35–40 minutes, until the pastry is golden and the fruit is bubbling. Serve it warm or cold, with crème fraîche, ice cream or cold, thick cream.

VARIATIONS

- In autumn and winter, I often make this with rhubarb or poached quince (see page 122).
- Sometimes I add finely grated orange zest to the pastry and to the fruit filling, for a little added zing.

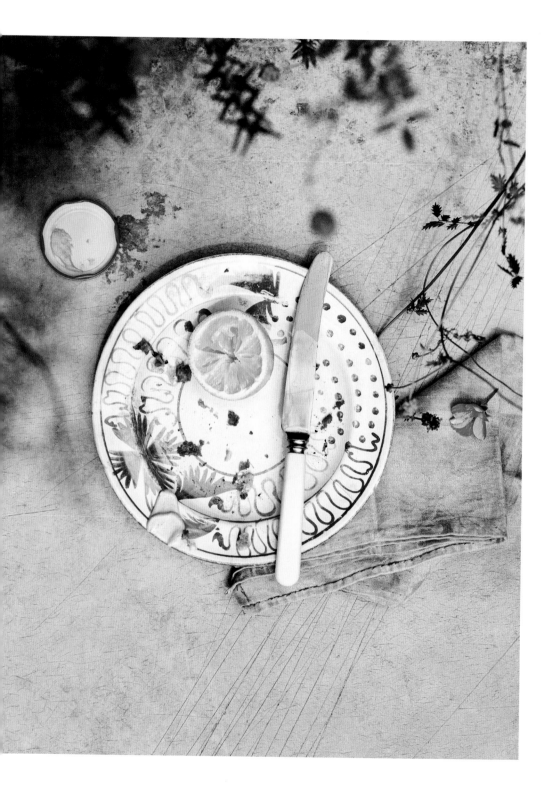

UnInstagrammable, that's what you are

I ONCE HAD A BOYFRIEND WHO HATED ALL FORMS OF BROWN FOOD and would sulk operatically if a casserole were ever placed in front of him, which was quite dramatic for a lad from Hendon. In the taxi on the way to dinner, he would ask if I thought our hosts might be '*stew* people' followed swiftly by, 'Do you think they're *dog* people?' – another prejudice. All I can say is that he was profoundly charming and clever, and if you're not going to experiment in your early twenties, then when? In the end, I married a man who both loves dogs and snaps wide awake at the crack of dawn with worry that we're already too late to put on the slow braise we plan to eat that night. Life is a wild ride.

Brown food is so rich in flavour, so comforting, and so often what we truly crave if we could only be honest with ourselves and shrug off the eye-candy influence of Instagram. Of course, we just used to call brown food 'food', before orange goji berries, scarlet pomegranates, emerald-green pistachios and fistfuls of torn coriander came along and pulled focus. In a world of smoothie bowls and rainbow bagels, stew needs to push hard to get to the front of the close-up queue, but some of the most delicious things I have ever eaten have been poor, obscure, plain and brown. Give me taste-ism over look-ism any day.

My friend Lucy has a freezer like a charnel house, filled with bones – particularly veal bones – ready to make gelatinous stock. A few years ago, social media and the good, old-fashioned print media were bubbling over with scathing opinions about the fashion for bone broth and the magical properties ascribed to it by certain influencers. I am not an enemy of bone broth. What is it but stock with notions? I am more like Lucy, who speaks of a twelve-hour-simmered *fond brun de veau* with holy reverence. When she announces on our WhatsApp group that she's about to commence a simmering, it's all I can do not to genuflect. Because not only is it pro-*fond*-ly good, but I believe firmly in the transformative properties of this 'delicious meat glue' (Lucy™), filled with collagen. Give me DMG any day, over Botox. Either on its own, sipped improvingly, or as a component of another dish, it is a savoury superstar.

Every second, every minute, every hour you simmer a slow-cooked dish, you concentrate its flavour, drag its umami notes out of hiding and into the light. Its flavour takes flight. The deep colour comes from time: slow, careful, mouth-watering time. Embrace it, celebrate it, serve it. Be a stew person. They are some of the best people alive, and the least troubled by wrinkles (NB Not a doctor).

Carbonnade de boeuf

SERVES ~ **6–8**

This is one of my favourite dishes in life: dark, rich, seductive, comforting, like an excellent and reliable husband. If it's cold outside, or you're feeling low, or you want to spoil your friends, or drag your family away from screens to the table, I can think of few finer dishes. It may feel like an awful lot of onions, but they're essential to the sauce's depth of flavour, adding a discernible edge of sweetness. If you can, buy your lardons in a large slab and cut them yourself, as the pre-cut ones are often a bit stingy. Serve the carbonnade with mashed potato, chips, baked potatoes, whatever your favourite potato might be, and buttered greens of some kind. It's even better cooked the day before if you have time.

1.8kg beef shoulder or chuck steak, cut into 3cm cubes

salt and freshly ground black pepper

2 tablespoons sunflower oil

40g unsalted butter, plus a little more for frying the pain d'épice

300g smoked lardons, cut into 1.5–2cm cubes ideally

4 onions, about 800g, halved and cut into thin slices

1 bay leaf

3 carrots, about 400g, cut on the slant into 5cm pieces

1 tablespoon light muscovado sugar

1.25 litres beer, ideally a Belgian beer such as Chimay Gold or Red, or Leffe Blonde

4 tablespoons cider vinegar

1 bouquet garni, comprising 1 bay leaf, a few fresh parsley stalks and 2 sprigs of fresh thyme tied together with kitchen string

2 whole cloves, or ¼ teaspoon ground cloves

2 tablespoons Dijon mustard (optional)

about 5–6 thick slices of pain d'épice or not-too-fiery gingerbread, depending on the size of your pan, plus one extra slice

a generous handful of fresh parsley leaves and fine stalks, about 15g, roughly chopped

Season the meat with salt and pepper, then warm the oil and half the butter in a large, heavy-bottomed saucepan or casserole (you need one with a lid) over a medium–high heat and sauté the beef, browning it all over. You'll need to do this in batches so you don't crowd the pan – if you overcrowd the pan it's hard to get them beautifully brown (see TIP, page 228). As pieces of the beef are cooked, remove them to a large plate. Once you've cooked the beef, repeat the process with the lardons, putting them on the plate too when they're lightly browned and have rendered some of their fat.

Chapter 9 ~ UnInstagrammable, that's what you are

Lower the heat, add the remaining butter and cook the onions. Add them to the pan with a good pinch of salt and a bay leaf and sauté them gently, stirring from time to time, until they're beautifully soft (they will be darkened because they will take on the delicious residue from cooking the meat, but you don't want to cook them so hard or so fast that they take on colour of their own. Be gentle with them and they will reward you). This will take about 40 minutes to do properly, which is of course what you want. Add the carrots and sauté for a further 5 minutes.

Next, sprinkle on the sugar and stir to dissolve and lightly caramelize, then return the meat and any juices that have accumulated on the plate to the pan. Pour in the beer and vinegar. Add the bouquet garni and cloves and season gently. Bring to a simmer. Spread the mustard on one side of the slices of pain d'épice – use just enough slices to cover the surface of the casserole, mustard side down. Lower the heat to the barest simmer and put the lid on. Simmer very, very gently over a low heat for 2 hours. If you prefer, you can put it into the oven at this point – 160°C/140°C fan/gas 3.

It's done when the meat is meltingly tender. Taste the sauce and add more salt and pepper if necessary. If the sauce is thin, remove the lid and simmer until thickened. Stir in the parsley.

Cut the remaining pain d'épice into rough cubes and sauté them in butter until golden. Serve scattered over the carbonnade, with some form of potatoes on the side and some cheerfully healthy greens, because, well, you know.

~

Rabbit with prunes

SERVES ~ 4

I can't tell you how many cabinets in how many kitchens I have almost set fire to, or how many smoke alarms I have set off, because of my love of flambéing. I will not be stopped. Not only do I live for the drama, but this extra step contributes an added depth of flavour to almost any sauce. It's really worth it.

You need to pit the prunes, and this is sometimes easier to do after they have been soaked in the wine. Serve this lovely dish simply with boiled potatoes or rice, and a sprightly green salad (see page 27).

200g prunes, the best you can find, pruneaux d'Agen for perfection, stones removed (see above)

250ml red wine

70g unsalted butter

200g unsmoked lardons

2 medium onions, about 350g, diced

1 bay leaf

salt and freshly ground black pepper

1 medium carrot, about 70g, diced

1 celery stick, about 50g, trimmed, any strings removed with a sharp vegetable peeler, and diced

4 tablespoons plain flour

1 wild rabbit, about 1.2kg, cut into 8 pieces – ask your butcher to do this for you if you're not confident about doing it yourself

4 tablespoons brandy or Calvados

700ml chicken or vegetable stock

1 bouquet garni, comprising a few stalks of fresh parsley, a bay leaf and a couple of sprigs of fresh thyme tied together with kitchen string

1 small bunch of fresh parsley, tough stalks removed, fine stalks and leaves roughly chopped, about 15g

2 tablespoons Dijon mustard

TO SERVE
boiled or mashed potatoes, or rice

Place the prunes in a bowl with 200ml of the wine and leave to soak for 2–4 hours. Drain, reserving the wine, and destone the prunes if you haven't done it already.

Melt 30g of the butter in a large, heavy-bottomed casserole or saucepan over a medium–high heat and sauté the lardons until they're golden and have rendered their fat. Reduce the heat to medium–low, add the onions, bay leaf and a pinch of salt and sauté gently, stirring from time to time, until the onions are very soft,

about 15 minutes. Add the carrot and celery and sauté for a further 5 minutes. Turn off the heat, then use a spatula to scrape everything from the pan into a bowl and set aside for the moment.

In a low-sided dish, whisk together the flour and 1 teaspoon each of salt and pepper, then dip each piece of rabbit into the seasoned flour, shaking off any excess.

Return the pan to the heat and melt the remaining butter over a medium–high heat. Brown the rabbit in batches, until each piece is golden all over. When you're done, put all the meat back into the pan.

In a small pan, or a heatproof jug in the microwave, warm the brandy and then carefully set fire to it, pour it into the pan and flambé the rabbit. When the flames die down, lower the heat a bit and return the lardons and vegetables to the pan with the rabbit. Pour in the wine reserved from the prunes and the stock, and add the bouquet garni. Simmer very gently, partially covered, for an hour. Add the prunes and simmer for a further 40 minutes to an hour, until the rabbit is very tender. Taste and add more salt and pepper if it needs it. Remove it from the heat, fish out the bouquet garni, stir in the parsley and mustard and serve with potatoes or rice.

~

Mushroom ragù

SERVES ~ 6

I know this feels like a lot of mushrooms, but mushrooms are second only to spinach in their miraculous capacity to shrink in the pan.

25g dried porcini mushrooms

3 tablespoons olive oil

2 shallots, diced

1 small celery stick, about 35g, trimmed, any tough strings removed with a sharp vegetable peeler, and finely diced (5mm pieces)

1 small carrot, about 35g, finely diced (5mm pieces)

3 fresh thyme sprigs

1 bay leaf

salt and freshly ground black pepper

800g chestnut mushrooms, sliced about 5mm thick

→

4 cloves of garlic, halved, green germ removed, and very finely chopped

250ml white wine

2 tablespoons concentrated tomato purée

1 × 400g tin of cherry tomatoes

1 tablespoon white wine vinegar or cider vinegar

½ teaspoon sugar

a good pinch of chilli flakes

a small bunch of fresh parsley, tough stalks removed, fine stalks and leaves chopped, about 15g

360g dried pappardelle pasta

Parmesan cheese, grated, for serving

Put the porcini into a small bowl with 500ml of just-warm water. Leave them to soak for at least 30 minutes while you get on with the rest. When you're ready to use them, use a slotted spoon gently to lift them out of the bowl, leaving any sand or grit behind, and rinse them in a sieve to remove any last bits. Put them to one side. Line the sieve with kitchen paper or muslin and strain the liquid into a jug – keep it for later.

In a heavy-bottomed casserole or pan, warm the oil over a medium–low heat and sauté the shallots, celery and carrot with the thyme sprigs, bay leaf and a good pinch of salt until softened, about 10 minutes. Raise the heat a bit, add the chestnut mushrooms and sprinkle on 1 teaspoon of salt. Cook them quite hard and hot (as for the garlicky tarragon mushrooms, page 152). Once they begin to release their liquid, cook them, stirring quite often, until the liquid evaporates and the mushrooms begin to take on a little colour, which should take about 15 minutes. Don't stint at this stage: a soggy, undercooked mushroom is a terrible disappointment. Lower the heat and add the garlic and the drained porcini and stir for a minute more. Pour in the wine and simmer for a few minutes until the liquid is reduced to a third, then spoon in the tomato purée and give everything a stir. Add the tinned tomatoes, the reserved soaking water from the porcini, the vinegar, 1 teaspoon of freshly ground black pepper, the sugar and chilli flakes and let the ragù simmer gently, uncovered, for about 50 minutes (at about minute 35, think about putting the pasta on), until the sauce is rich, glossy and thick. Stir in the parsley. Taste and add more salt and pepper if necessary; remember you want the ragù to be quite intense, as the flavour must carry through the pasta. Fish out the bay leaf and the thyme sprigs.

Bring a large pan of water to the boil and add plenty of salt (see TIP, page 254). Cook the pappardelle according to the instructions on the packet. Drain it well and toss it with the sauce. Serve immediately, in warmed bowls, with Parmesan grated generously over the top.

~

Chapter 10

~

What food writers really eat, mostly toast

WHEN I'M ON A DEADLINE, I LIVE ON TOAST. I know lots of other food writers do too. I can't break the honour code of the sorority here, but it's something we discuss secretly over lively dinners or in the intimate confessional of the WhatsApp group. Occasionally, we break cover and mention it on Twitter, before once again retreating behind *the mise en place*, slightly embarrassed and ashamed. And also worried in case no one will ever commission us again. We may be writing about making your own biang biang noodles from scratch or developing the foolproof recipe for a croquembouche, but all the while we are spreading butter thickly on crisp, hot toast and calling it lunch. And personally at least – in the interests of full disclosure – that bread is as likely to be industrial sliced white as it is mouth-lacerating artisanal sourdough that I coaxed into being myself.

When he was about six, on his infant school's open day, my younger brother, Grahame, proudly showed my parents his contribution to a class project. The children were encouraged to write and draw something under the heading 'My Mammy'. Other children wrote about how pretty their mothers were, or how kind or good at knitting. Grahame wrote: 'My mammy is a very good cook, but it is mostly beans on toast.' Well done for telling the truth, kid. Toast and something from a tin, or a poached egg, that's what made us.

As a student, toast got me through hangovers and heartbreak, essay crises and penury. On your worst days, toast is something you can offer visitors when you have precious little else. It is the culinary equivalent of its natural companion, a nice cup of tea: a balm, a comfort, a bargain. Today, my best days start as I wake to the smell of coffee and toast wafting up the stairs, marmalade for me, Marmite for Séan. He almost always makes the breakfast. Yes, I don't know why I got so lucky after so many fixer-upper boyfriends either. I choose not to question it, as I brush toast crumbs off the duvet and launch myself into the day.

While bargain-basement simple toast cannot be bettered, sometimes I want to fancy it up a bit because I can't help myself, and because it's nice to give toast the chance to step up from understudy to star. So in this chapter, I give you my pixied-up toast, and even toast pudding with fruit and cheese. But however you make it, in lunch as in life, make sure you spread the butter all the way to the edges.

Upside-down French onion soup

SERVES ~ 2 as a main course, 4 as a starter on 4 smaller pieces of bread

I invented this dish because while I absolutely love French onion soup, I cannot be trusted to eat it in polite company. I can barely even be trusted to eat it on my own. I am quite clumsy and invariably end up with half of it down my top and strings of melted cheese on my chin. So I created this version (apologies to my dry cleaner's accountant), which takes all the great elements of the soup, allows you to eat it with a knife and fork, and ensures you can survive lunch with your dignity more or less intact. The quantities here are big enough for a whole meal with a salad, or make smaller ones to serve as starters. Be warned, it's a lot of cheese, but when it comes to cheese I have no off switch. You might want a little less. Or you might want a little more, in which case, if we are ever in the same room, please introduce yourself.

40g unsalted butter

1 bay leaf

a sprig of fresh thyme

2 medium onions, about 350–400g total weight, halved and finely sliced

a pinch of sugar

salt and freshly ground black pepper

200ml good, rich beef or chicken stock*

1 tablespoon Cognac (optional)

2 large slices of decent bread, about 1.5cm thick

130g Gruyère or Comté cheese, or a combination of the two, grated

*If I haven't got homemade stock in the freezer, I use one of the excellent little 200ml pouches of demi-glace beef and veal stock from Waitrose.

Melt the butter in a frying pan over a medium heat, add the bay leaf and thyme and stir for a minute. Add the onions, sugar and a pinch of salt, and stir. Lower the heat, cover with a lid and cook for 15 minutes. Remove the lid, raise the heat a little and sauté gently for a further 20 minutes or so, stirring frequently, until the onions are very soft and a rich, golden brown. Add the stock and the Cognac if you are using it and simmer over a medium heat until most of the liquid has evaporated and you have a very thick, jammy mixture, about 10 minutes. Remove the bay leaf and thyme and add more salt and some pepper if it needs it.

While the onion mixture is cooking, heat up the grill and toast the bread on both sides – you want the slices to be quite well browned. Line a baking sheet with

Silpat or aluminium foil, place the toasts on the sheet and divide the onion mixture between the slices. Sprinkle the cheese on top, place under the grill and cook until golden and bubbling, then serve immediately.

TIP HOW TO FRY ONIONS IN REAL LIFE

I am generally an even-tempered person, but when I see recipes that say, 'Fry the onions until soft and translucent, about 5 minutes,' or, worse, 'Fry the onions until caramelized, about 15 minutes,' I want to give the writer a swift clunk about the head with a Le Creuset pan. No. Frying onions properly takes time. Building up flavour takes time. Skimpy timings in recipes are done to fool you into thinking you can get that dish on the table super-quickly, and then when it doesn't taste as good as you hope it's going to taste there's a natural inclination to think you've done something wrong. You haven't. They're fibbing. Here's what you need to know. To give yourself a head start, try to ensure the onions are chopped evenly so they will cook at the same speed, but don't stress out about that too much. My knife skills are fairly terrible, but somehow I muddle along. To achieve translucent onions, cook them over a medium–low heat, stirring frequently, until they are very soft but haven't taken on any colour. This should take about 15 minutes. For golden onions, turn up the heat a little to medium, keep stirring so they colour evenly, and keep going for about 20 minutes. Caramelized onions can take about 45 minutes to an hour, depending on the quantity and the size of the pan. Adding a pinch of salt helps to break down the cell walls in the onions so they cook more quickly and are less inclined to burn. Another tip I learned cooking alongside chefs in professional kitchens is that almost whatever you're making will benefit from the further punch of flavour you can achieve by adding a bay leaf or two, or a few sprigs of thyme, to the onions as you sauté them.

~

Garlicky tarragon mushrooms on toast

SERVES ~ 2

Proper, hot, hard frying gives great flavour to the most bog-standard, corner-shop mushrooms. Show them who's boss. I often have these mushrooms on toast for a quick lunch, or alternatively I fold them into an omelette or toss them through pasta. However you use them, this is very quick and good.

30g unsalted butter

2 tablespoons olive oil

1 bay leaf

500g chestnut or other mushrooms, cleaned (see **TIP**), and halved or sliced if huge

salt and freshly ground black pepper

4 cloves of garlic, halved, green germ removed, and very finely chopped

125ml white wine or dry vermouth

4 tablespoons crème fraîche

1 tablespoon Dijon mustard

6 spring onions, trimmed and thinly chopped

3 tablespoons roughly chopped fresh tarragon leaves

TO SERVE
very hot toast

Warm the butter, oil and bay leaf in a large frying pan over a medium–high heat. When the butter stops foaming, toss in the mushrooms and a good pinch of salt. Stir to coat, then raise the heat – you want to hear the mushrooms squeaking. They'll start to give up their moisture – keep cooking and stirring until this has evaporated and the mushrooms take on some colour, which will take about 8–10 minutes. Add the garlic and stir for a minute. Pour in the wine and cook until it's almost evaporated (this might be the moment when you want to make the toast). Discard the bay leaf. Remove from the heat and stir in the crème fraîche, mustard, spring onions and tarragon. Season with salt and pepper and serve immediately, on hot toast.

TIP HOW TO CLEAN MUSHROOMS

They are thirsty little beasts and the wetter you get them, the harder they become to cook properly, so keep them parched. Simply wipe them with some damp kitchen paper, or, if they are quite dirty, put them into a colander, run them very, very quickly under a cold tap, then rub them dry with kitchen paper or a clean tea towel. If you have intricate little mushrooms like girolles, brush off any dust or woodland debris. You can buy special brushes for this, but a pastry brush works just as well.

Roquefort, figs and honey on brioche

SERVES ~ **1–2**

Sometimes I just want toast 'pudding', and that's when I pull out the brioche or challah and pile on the fruit . . . I use figs here, but this is great with nectarines and peaches too, or a combination of fruit. I like to use quite a savoury, herby honey for this, chestnut honey ideally, but warming the honey with the herbs helps add flavour if you are using a fairly neutral one.

2 tablespoons honey (see above)

1 sprig of fresh lemon thyme, plus some leaves for serving

2–3 figs, halved

a little sunflower oil, for the grill pan

2 thick slices of brioche or challah

80–100g Roquefort

a few hazelnuts, toasted (see page 258) and roughly chopped

In a small pan (or in the microwave), warm the honey with the thyme until just simmering around the edges. Brush the cut side of the figs with the honey, and reserve the rest.

Heat a ridged grill pan ideally – gotta love those grill lines – or a small, non-stick pan over a medium–high heat and brush with the barest amount of oil, then place the figs on the grill pan, cut side down. Heat for a couple of minutes until the figs are warmed through and caramelized – be careful not to let it go so far that they burn, you just want a good char on them. Put them to one side while you toast the bread. Place the toast on a plate or plates, put the figs on top and crumble on the Roquefort. Scatter over the hazelnuts and a few of the thyme leaves, then trickle on the remaining honey and eat immediately.

~

Chapter 11

~

Bone appétit!

ONE BONE-COLD SUNDAY MORNING FIFTEEN YEARS AGO, Séan and I pitched up at Finsbury Park with a thermos of spiked coffee and a wiry, wriggling puppy the size of a small brown loaf. I felt very underfleeced and inappropriately shod in my stone-coloured mac and shiny brown leather boots. This was Barney's first puppy class and it wasn't only the dogs that were barking.

As we stood in a loose circle being lectured on the importance of good recall, a rather tightly wound woman in a quilted jacket pulled from her pocket a small plastic tub of something revolting. Its death-smell permeated the chill air, despite the fumes coming from my café Cognac. Her tiny poodle looked on with adoration, seated, laser-eyed, until given the command, 'Here you are!' Only then did the puppy creep forward and snaffle the death-smell treat whole. The woman caught me looking at her. Barney, like me, has precious little concept of delayed gratification and a fairly patchy attitude to obedience. 'Dried liver treats. Organic. I make them myself.' Of course you do.

On the way home, I said to Séan, 'If I ever turn into the kind of woman who cooks for her dog, shoot me.'

Many years later, all I can say is that he is either an exceptionally kind and patient man or possibly just quite forgetful. I now cook for both our dogs, Barney and Gracie, and for the cat, Dixie. I've even written books about it. I have special containers just for them, an extra-large stock pot for simmering all those chickens, and yes, a dehydrator for making irresistible (to them) dried offal-y morsels which smell so terrible I am astonished none of our neighbours has contacted the local forensics unit. I pay attention to their likes and dislikes, just as I would with anyone who was eating at my table (rather than under it). I've come to embrace the fact that one of my dogs eschews all cheese but Cheddar, and the other chews shoes.

I suppose I shouldn't be so surprised at this wholesome turn of events. If I love you, I cook for you. If you come to my house, I cook for you. I can't help it. The American writer Edith Wharton described her little dog as 'a heartbeat at my feet'. It is as natural for me to decipher what pleases these tiny heartbeats, these constant companions, who see me at my worst and love me anyway, as it would be if it were you, walking into my house and curling up on the rug, trusting me with your life, or at least with your dinner. It is a very small price to pay for occasionally being allowed to sleep in my favourite spot in the bed or to occupy the most comfortable chair – all of it, I mean, not just a slightly awkward corner. As you see, the discipline training has gone well over all these years. No one knows who the genuine Alpha occupants of our house are, and honestly I like it better that way. Organic liver treat, anyone? Fleece optional. I don't judge.

Chicken and apple shoes for Gracie

MAKES ~ about 24, depending on the size of the cutter

I make these biscuits for my dog Gracie, to act as a decoy for human shoes. I bought a special, shoe-shaped cutter for them because I am that idiot, but you can use any smallish cutter you like. I've even used the metal cap off a bottle of olive oil quite successfully, to cut out neat, small Scooby snacks, the perfect size to put in your pocket and take on a walk. Malt extract is rich in beneficial enzymes and antioxidants and also makes them taste nice, but leave it out if you don't want to buy a big jar just for the dog (what kind of monster are you?).

200g boneless, skinless, joyless chicken breast, poached

150g rolled oats

100g apple sauce, unsweetened, or 100g grated apple

100g buckwheat flour, plus a little more for dusting

1 tablespoon malt extract (optional)

about 50ml hot water

Preheat the oven to 180°C/160°C fan/gas 4. Line two baking sheets with non-stick baking parchment or Silpat.

Blitz everything together in a food processor or with a stick blender to make a firm dough, adding a little hot water if necessary.

Turn it out on to some baking parchment or cling film lightly dusted with flour, pat it out into a loose round, then roll it out to 5mm thick with a lightly floured rolling pin. Cut out the dough, rolling out any scraps and cutting out more biscuits until you have used up all the dough. Arrange them on the baking sheets and bake for 35–40 minutes, until slightly golden and hard. Remove them from the oven and leave them to cool completely on the trays.

They will keep in a sealed container in the fridge for a week, or in the freezer for three months.

~

Cheddar and parsley bones for Barney

MAKES ~ **about 24, depending on the size of the cutter**

These are a good way to use up dried-out ends of cheese, and the parsley helps to sweeten the dog's breath. Hopefully.

250g buckwheat flour

about 120g fresh parsley, finely chopped, stalks and all

1 large carrot, about 120g, grated

60g Cheddar cheese, finely grated

½ teaspoon brewer's yeast (optional)

50ml olive oil or coconut oil

about 100ml hot water

Preheat the oven to 180°C/160°C fan/gas 4. Line two baking sheets with non-stick baking parchment or Silpat.

In a large bowl, stir together the flour, parsley, carrot, Cheddar and brewer's yeast if you're using it until everything is very well combined. Sprinkle on the oil and stir, then add just enough hot water to make a stiff dough. Turn the dough out on to some baking parchment or cling film lightly dusted with flour, pat it out into a loose round, then roll out to 5mm thick with a lightly floured rolling pin. Cut out the dough with your cutters, rolling out any scraps and cutting out biscuits until you have used up all the dough. Arrange them on the baking sheets and bake for 35–40 minutes, until slightly golden and hard. Remove them from the oven and leave them to cool completely on the trays.

They will keep in a sealed jar for a week, or in the freezer for three months.

~

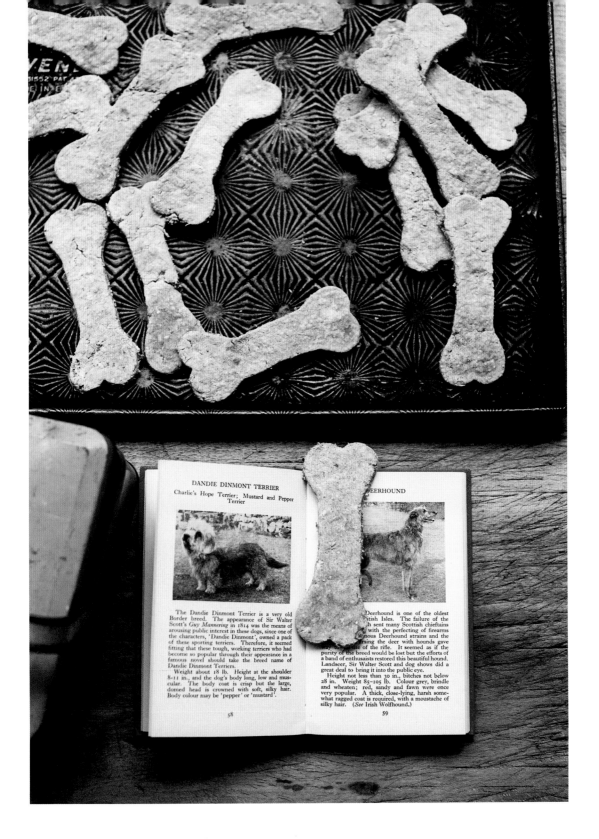

DANDIE DINMONT TERRIER

Charlie's Hope Terrier; Mustard and Pepper Terrier

DEERHOUND

The Dandie Dinmont Terrier is a very old Border breed. The appearance of Sir Walter Scott's *Guy Mannering* in 1814 was the means of arousing public interest in these dogs, since one of the characters, 'Dandie Dinmont', owned a pack of these sporting terriers. Therefore, it seemed fitting that these tough, working terriers who had become so popular through their appearance in a famous novel should take the breed name of Dandie Dinmont Terriers.

Weight about 18 lb. Height at the shoulder 8–11 in., and the dog's body long, low and muscular. The body coat is crisp but the large, domed head is crowned with soft, silky hair. Body colour may be 'pepper' or 'mustard'.

58

Deerhound is one of the oldest itish Isles. The failure of the h sent many Scottish chieftains y with the perfecting of firearms mous Deerhound strains and the rsing the deer with hounds gave e of the rifle. It seemed as if the purity of the breed would be lost but the efforts of a band of enthusiasts restored this beautiful hound. Landseer, Sir Walter Scott and dog shows did a great deal to bring it into the public eye.

Height not less than 30 in., bitches not below 28 in. Weight 85–105 lb. Colour grey, brindle and wheaten; red, sandy and fawn were once very popular. A thick, close-lying, harsh somewhat ragged coat is required, with a moustache of silky hair. (*See* Irish Wolfhound.)

59

Chapter 12

Marmalade days

I WAS ALWAYS PICKED LAST FOR GAMES AT SCHOOL, so it took me until later in life to discover my perfect team sport: cooking with friends. You chat, laugh, sing along terribly to country music, segue smoothly from coffee to cocktails, and then suddenly – bonus – dinner's ready and you all get to have a lovely sit down.

I am not very good at delegating, despite my encouraging you to do it at every possible opportunity. It's too late for me, but save yourselves (time). I am not proud to say that I have firm opinions about how carrots should be cut (on an angle) and beans prepped (topped, never tailed), for example, but my desire to ensure everyone's happy and living their best lives requires me to say, 'Oh, that's how you do it. That's fine, of course.' We both know it's not, but you have a knife in your hand and let's just all move on.

But despite this pass-agg carrots-and-beans talk, I do have friends who I can rely on to make the salad, others who are brilliant at grilling, or making puddings, in the same way sporty types know who is the best striker, defender or midfielder. I've bottled hundreds of jars of pickles and jams with my friend

Vanessa (her chutney's on page 166), the windows running with condensation as we scooped ladles of preserves into warmed jars and worked out the perplexing challenge of how to plant up a shady corner or what colour to paint a north-facing wall. I've made hundreds and hundreds of tiny bread rolls with my friend Julia, to serve with ham and pimento cheese (page 171) at her annual summer party or at one of the evenings during the year when she sells her glorious ceramics – they look as though they've been pulled from deep under the sea, but are very glad to hold your lemons or tomatoes on your kitchen counter for now.

One of my favourite days of the year is the one when Julia and I make marmalade. She's from Tennessee, so she wasn't born to marmalade, but she's taken to it so enthusiastically she must have some Dundee in her somewhere. We settle into my kitchen with crates of citrus and bottles of booze, and get to slicing, macerating and simmering, in a kitchen so steamy our complexions are much improved for our efforts, and the view of the garden is obscured by a voile of condensation. (One of these years, I will invest in decent extraction, but there are always more important things to spend the money on that are cheaper and require less research, like a car, a house, or one of the smaller Scottish islands.) Oh, and the booze is mostly to stir into the marmalade at the end of its cooking. Those lines are sometimes blurred.

You don't even have to cook to be part of my kitchen squad. My friend Victoria, the sister of my heart, has spent many afternoons in my kitchen, me hauling things in and out of the oven, her flipping through the paper, reading out choice bits, as we both form hasty but strong opinions on everything from cabinet reshuffles to kaftans, yes or no? When her sons Luca and Leo were very small, we'd prop them up on kitchen stools, draped in hastily fashioned tea-towel aprons to do distracting washing-up, so we could continue the conversation we began on a journalism course thirty years ago and haven't stopped since.

I think the intimacy of the kitchen confessional has magical properties. You know those times you go on a car ride with someone you care about and it's suddenly easier to have the conversation you've been stalling on for ages? I think that happens because you're side-by-side rather than face-to-face. It's freeing. You gaze out of the window and tongues become untied, thoughts fall more easily from your lips. The kitchen is the same. In the midst of gentle industry, shoulder to shoulder at the stove, there is an ease to conversation. The stories we tell each other while we're doing other things, these chopping-board tales, make and reinforce friendships, deepen connection, just as much as sitting round a table. And, as an added bonus, you're guaranteed marmalade.

Vanessa's De Beauvoir chutney

MAKES ~ 5 × 500g jars

My friend Vanessa is one of the best natural cooks I know, and certainly one of the most hospitable. We've thrown so many parties together, at my house or hers, spending hours standing side by side at the kitchen counter, prepping and chopping, talking and drinking wine. Today, she lives in Puglia, but when we can't physically be together, we still cook together via running commentaries on WhatsApp and Zoom.

A few years ago, before she decamped to Italy, she created this excellent chutney, which she sold via the De Beauvoir Deli in Southgate Road, Islington. She says, 'This one takes a whole morning of chopping, so pull up a chair, put the radio on or invite over a friend who's equally dedicated and arm yourself with your sharpest knife . . .' Vanessa makes this with malt vinegar, which is punchy, and I make it with cider vinegar, which obviously has a milder flavour. That about sums us up, really.

1 large cauliflower, florets neatly chopped so they retain their nice shape, 750g–1kg prepared weight (save the leaves and roast them, see TIP, page 68)

850ml brown malt vinegar or cider vinegar

1 medium swede, about 600g, cut into 1cm dice

3 medium courgettes, about 500g, cut into 1cm dice

3 apples, about 450g, unpeeled, cored and cut into 1cm dice

4 medium carrots, about 300g, cut into 1cm dice

2 medium onions, about 300g, finely diced

20 cornichons, about 80g, finely chopped

6 fat, sticky dates, about 150g, stoned and chopped – I use Medjool for this, which seems like an extravagance, but you want them to be juicy

6 cloves of garlic, halved, green germ removed, and very finely chopped

380g dark muscovado sugar

4 tablespoons lemon juice

2 teaspoons mustard seeds

2 teaspoons ground allspice

1 teaspoon cayenne pepper

1 teaspoon salt

Make sure all your jars are sterilized (see TIP, page 79) and have vinegar-proof lids.

Combine all the ingredients in a large, non-reactive pan. It doesn't have to be a preserving pan, but it should be stainless steel or enamelled cast iron, not aluminium, which reacts badly with vinegar. It will feel like not enough vinegar, but it is. Stir gently over a medium heat to dissolve the sugar. Once the sugar has dissolved, bring it to a gentle boil and cook, stirring often, until the vegetables are cooked but retain a little crunch. They'll continue to cook and soften a bit as they cool. The mixture should be glossy and thick – a wooden spoon dragged across the bottom of the pan should make the ingredients part for a couple of seconds before coming back together.

Let the chutney cool for 5 minutes before ladling it into the warm, sterilized jars (a wide-mouthed jam funnel will help), ensuring there are no air bubbles. Screw on the lids loosely and when cool, tighten them up and label the jars, including the date. The flavour improves over time, so store for a couple of months in a cool, dark, dry place before eating it, and once opened, store in the fridge and eat within a couple of weeks. Unopened jars will keep for a year. I'm saying that because that is the correct thing to say, but I have eaten chutney which has been kept well and was several years old and it was fine and I am fine.

TIP
Break the cauliflower into neat florets, but not so small that they will break down to nothing as they cook. The other vegetables can be cut into a smallish, neat dice of about 1cm. This means they cook at roughly the same rate, and also that they look good and have a better texture when you serve them.

~

Negroni marmalade (because, come on)

MAKES ~ 9 × 200ml jars

The Negroni is my favourite winter cocktail, so it's perhaps a tipsily logical development to pair it with that other hero of the cold months, marmalade. The bitterness of the alcohol is a good counterbalance to the sweetness of the blood oranges, which are less sharp than Sevilles. This works very well with Sevilles too – the resulting marmalade is more tart, but none the worse for that. You certainly know you're awake.

1kg unwaxed blood oranges

2 lemons – enough for 100ml juice

1 teaspoon salt

2 litres water

1.5kg granulated sugar

30ml Campari

30ml gin

30ml sweet red vermouth

Wash the fruit well. Halve the oranges and lemons and juice them. Pour the juice into a large bowl, and put the pips from both the oranges and the lemons into a separate bowl. Pull the papery membranes from the juiced halves with your fingers. Scraping with a teaspoon sometimes helps – I have an old grapefruit spoon with a serrated edge which appeared from I know not where in our cutlery drawer and is enormously useful for all manner of things, apart from eating grapefruit. Put the membranes into the small bowl with the pips. Lay out a piece of muslin about 20cm square, tip in the pips and membranes, and tie up with kitchen string into a little pectin-rich bundle.

With a sharp knife, cut the orange peel into strips. I think thin strips work best with blood oranges, but this is entirely a matter of choice. Put the strips into the large bowl with the orange juice and lemon juice. Add the muslin bundle, the salt and the water, cover and leave overnight to soak, or for up to 24 hours.

When you're ready to make the marmalade, transfer the mixture to a large, heavy-bottomed stainless steel pan or a preserving pan. Remove the muslin bag and squeeze it firmly over the pan so that as much pectin as possible goes back into the fruit. Bring to a simmer and cook for 1½–2 hours, until the peel is very soft and pulls apart easily. Once you add the sugar, it won't get any softer so it is important not to be too hasty at this stage.

Sterilize your jars, jug, ladle and jam funnel (see TIP, page 79) and put some saucers into the freezer to chill.

Begin to add the sugar to the pan, about a quarter at a time, stirring until each addition is dissolved before adding more. Increase the heat, bring to a rolling boil, and boil for about 12–15 minutes until it reaches a setting point. A little of the marmalade dropped on to a chilled saucer and left for a minute should wrinkle when pushed with a finger.

Remove the pan from the heat and leave to cool for 5 minutes. Add the Campari, gin and vermouth and stir. Ladle the marmalade into the jug and pour it into the hot jars, or just use a jam funnel if you have one, and a ladle. Fill to the brim and immediately seal with the lids. Turn the jars upside down for a minute – this helps to ensure a good seal – then turn them the right way up and leave to cool. When you label the jars, make sure you include the date. The marmalade will keep in a cool, dry, dark cupboard for a couple of years.

TIP

A tiny amount of this marmalade is wonderful stirred into a Negroni, or used in the base of a sponge pudding, or as a glaze for duck or ham.

~

Julia's pimento cheese

SERVES ~ a crowd, depending on what else you are serving with it

My friend Julia and I bonded over our shared love of cheese (truthfully, our shared terror of the snooty owners of our local posh cheese shop, but that's a tale for another day), so it's particularly appropriate that she introduced me to pimento cheese. It's a classic party dish of the American South and part of Julia's Chattanooga heritage. This recipe comes from Brenda, a family friend from Lookout Mountain, Tennessee, who carefully wrote out the recipe on an index card, and it has now passed from Brenda's kitchen to Julia's to mine, in that comforting daisy chain of deliciousness, one cook to another.

I've stood shoulder to shoulder with Julia in her kitchen more times than I can count but not as many as I would like, preparing pimento cheese, arranging plates of crackers and celery, folding thick slices of ham into tiny yeasted rolls, helping her to get ready for her summer party or for one of the sales she has of the beautiful ceramics she makes. Pure happiness.

The pimento in the title is grilled red pepper – I use the flame-grilled ones you get in jars.

340g mature, strong Cheddar cheese, grated

340g mild Cheddar cheese, grated

225g jarred, flame-grilled red peppers, finely chopped

1½ tablespoons sweet paprika, smoked or unsmoked, depending on your taste

1 tablespoon white balsamic vinegar

1½ tablespoons sweet pickle juice, from the jar

1 teaspoon caster sugar

1 teaspoon salt

4 dashes Tabasco sauce, or more according to your taste

300g good, creamy mayonnaise, such as Stokes or Tracklements

TO SERVE
celery sticks, crackers or crostini

Mix everything together well, taste and adjust the seasoning if necessary, and serve on a platter with crudités and crackers. That's it.

TIP
Pimento cheese makes an excellent sandwich, and a spectacular grilled cheese, especially with a little finely chopped spring onion or shallot added to the mix.

~

Chapter 13

How to be a farmer in the privacy of your own kitchen

MOST OF US CAN'T GROW EVERYTHING WE EAT, but many of us can grow some of it. I'm the laziest gardener alive, but the herbs and other idiot-proof edibles I grow in my kitchen, or just by the back door, or in my little garden itself, add sprightly flavour to my cooking every single day. My horticultural expertise is just a slightly grown-up version of growing cress on cotton wool. I am very much of the 'What have you got to lose?' school of gardening, where I haphazardly assign plants to spare pots and bare spots in the soil and hope for the best. I do, I am afraid, have an 'If they die, they die' approach – I get to enjoy them while they live, and they can usually be replaced for not much more than the price of a lacklustre packet of supermarket herbs. And I am quite unstoppable in my lust for plants. In my characteristically Cancerian way of making your home wherever you are, when we rent somewhere for more than a week in the summer I often create a miniature herb garden with plants from a local market or nursery. My favourite possible thing about holidays is pretending that I live there, and this is just the green-fingered part of that.

I read gardening books and plant catalogues like novels, particularly in the winter when the days are short and the grubbing about in the soil opportunities are limited. When someone gave me Jekka McVicar's *Complete Herb Book* I sat with it a few evenings, larding it generously with Post-it notes. I was entranced as much by the poetry as the plants. How can you not grow tarragon when you know its name means 'little dragon'? Of course, myrtle is good with pork, but it was also sacred to the goddess Aphrodite. I adore fennel, and not just because it is said that it will prevent ghosts from entering a building if you place fronds in a keyhole. You can't be too careful.

Today I mostly buy my herbs from Mick and Sylvia Grover's stall at Columbia Road market, by mail order from Pepperpot Nursery, from Jekka's own mail order service, and from Mark Diacono of Otter Farm.

Years ago, I helped Mark with the recipes for his book *A Taste of the Unexpected*. As well as being a grower of delicious things, he's a wonderfully inventive cook. I find these two traits often go together. It's a short distance between growing a wigwam of peas and inventing ways to eat them, and between cooking peas and wondering how easy it might be to grow them. From him, I also learned that if you have limited time and space, to concentrate on the things which are difficult to buy and add an extra KAPOW! in the kitchen.

So by the back door, I grow a little emergency parsley, but I also supplement it with fat bunches from the Turkish greengrocer. I use far too much of it to keep up. Ditto coriander, plus it bolts quicker than Usain. While I grow a few lettuces, the occasional hanging basket of cherry tomatoes or tub of lively courgettes, the Antonio Carluccio principle of MOF MOF – minimum of effort, maximum of flavour – that I write about in Chapter 8 means I mostly grow herbs, lots of them, pots and pots of them. So yes, bay leaves, several kinds of basil, French tarragon, chives, lots of different mints for teas and syrups and lamb chops, several varieties of thyme, a couple of sages, oregano and marjoram, fennel, and deliciously sherbet-y lemon verbena. But also salad burnet for its cucumber-coolness in salads and drinks, lovage to add to chicken and pork and to chop into omelettes, summer and winter savory to add to beans, mushrooms and lamb . . . And one of the added benefits of growing your own is that you also get to use the flowers and, in the case of fennel, the pollen, which is just beyond chic. Oh this? I grew it myself.

You can also use them extravagantly, as herbs invariably should be used, knowing that the more you cut them the more vigorously they will grow. Stir them into things, throw them over the top, or in the case of parsley, mint and coriander (and others, these are just the most obvious) arrange them in lush abundance on platters of vegetables or cooked meat. This is common in cuisines from the Ukraine to Iran, and it is such a beautiful, generous, uplifting thing to do. Use them and eat them lavishly. I often arrange bunches and small pots of herbs along the table in place of flowers – much cheaper, but no less elegant and charming.

I always have a few pots of herbs in the kitchen too, just in case I'm too idle to go outside (reader, I am often too idle). In winter, I bring some of the more tender herbs inside in an effort to keep them going a little bit longer and to profit more easily from their deliciousness.

For their size and the effort it takes to cultivate them, herbs add an unsurpassed vitality to cooking and make you feel like a proper gardener, when mostly what you're doing is wandering about in your pyjamas, cup of coffee in one hand, pair of scissors in the other, dreaming of dishes and little dragons and fennel pushed into keyholes.

Salsa verde

SERVES ~ a crowd, depending on what else you serve with it

Sometimes I put cornichons and a dab of mustard in my salsa verde, sometimes lemon zest and juice in place of the vinegar if I'm serving it with fish, sometimes I leave out the garlic or add more, depending on my mood. Sometimes I add mint, tarragon or coriander, sometimes I don't. You get the idea. But I try to keep roughly to the ratio of herbs, acid and other bits and pieces I describe here. I make it by chopping it by hand, but if I'm in a tearing rush and plan to serve it immediately, I sometimes just whiz it all together in my trusty mini chopper. It's best served straight away, but will keep in the fridge for 2 or 3 days sealed in a jar with a slick of olive oil over the top.

a big bunch of fresh parsley, tough stalks removed but you can leave the fine stalks on, about 50g

a smaller bunch of fresh basil, about 30g

6 anchovies (if in salt, give them a quick rinse), roughly chopped

1 tablespoon capers, rinsed and chopped

1 clove of garlic, halved, germ removed, and chopped

1 teaspoon Dijon mustard

1 tablespoon red wine vinegar

80–100ml extra virgin olive oil

salt and freshly ground black pepper

Put the herbs on a chopping board and, with a sharp knife, chop them together until they're quite fine. Put them into a pestle and mortar with the anchovies, capers and garlic and pound everything until smooth. Add the mustard and red wine vinegar, and then the oil in a slow, steady stream as you bash everything together into a vibrant green sauce. Taste and add more vinegar and some salt and pepper if it needs it.

TIP WHAT TO DO WITH YOUR SALSA VERDE
- This green sauce of dreams is infinitely versatile. If I make a batch at the weekend, I use it to cheer up all manner of leftovers and odds and ends at the beginning of the week.
- It's wonderful with simply cooked fish or squid, steak or roast chicken.
- Toss it through warm new potatoes.
- Swirl some through a simple bean soup.
- Add some to poached eggs on sourdough toast.

~

Chapter 14

~

Cake will save you

I WONDER IF YOU ARE LIKE ME? 'Cream together the butter and sugar' has the same soothing effect on me now that 'Once upon a time' had on me when I was a child. My shoulders drop. My breathing steadies. My heart stops pounding in my chest. Sometimes, when I don't know what to do, I bake. When I need to think something through, I bake. When I am sad, when I am happy, when I am procrastinating, I bake. It's interesting that our shared response to the onset of the coronavirus was to bake banana bread as though we were cooking up the miraculous vaccine itself.

In the past decade, we've all gone baking bonkers and I worry we've lost sight of the delights of the good, plain cake which, let's face it, is often the most comforting and delicious of all. This is in part the *Bake Off* effect, where a showstopper is for telly, not for tea. All hail these doughty, doughy souls, with their biscuit chess sets, spinning croquembouche windmills and bread lions with rosemary whiskers and almond claws, but I genuinely find competitive cooking programmes anxiety inducing. I don't want to watch people weep over cracked meringues, sunken tops and split custard. Life is tough enough. Besides, I have a nice, soothing murder mystery to watch on the Crime Channel.

It feels profoundly odd to me that we metaphorically carry bling bakers aloft, on a litter of biodynamic artisanal baguettes, because they can bake a cake that looks like a pomegranate, when actual pomegranates exist and are quite luscious, thank you very much. They are first-rate fruit, not second-rate cake.

In all this competitive cakery, we're at risk of forgetting the magic of a simple, old-fashioned cake. These over-elaborate crèmes fatales of the pâtisserie world, with their glitter and ganache, distract us from what cake can be, which is pleasure, joy even, and one of life's easy wins. In accepting our cakes' faults, their cracks and bubbles, their sunken middles and tough edges – not just accepting them, but embracing them and knowing that for all their flaws, they still make us smile – perhaps we can learn to embrace our own.

Plum cake

SERVES ~ 6–8

I am very keen on vanilla and mind terribly that its name has become synonymous with bland. It's anything but, and I think often recipes under-use it, as a background note, in the same way that people are often timid with salt. I want to know it's there. In this cake, I use vanilla sugar and vanilla extract, belt and braces.

This is a beautiful cake to make in late summer when plums are at their best. When you turn it out, it's shimmeringly beautiful, sticky with garnet fruit. I use almost any sweet pudding wine for this – I like a muscat – but when I'm in France I use Noilly Prat Ambré, their sweet vermouth which they annoyingly export only in the tiniest quantities. Its citrus, cardamom and vanilla notes are delicious with the fruit, so if you are ever in the same room as a bottle, do make this cake immediately.

You can serve this warm as a pudding, with cream or custard, or cold with crème fraîche (or whipped cream, or ice cream, or whatever you want really. I'm not the boss of you).

FOR THE PLUMS

5–6 plums, or enough to line a 23cm tin when halved, just ripe, not too soft

3 tablespoons demerara sugar

FOR THE CAKE

200g unsalted butter, room temperature, plus a little more for greasing the tin

*250g caster sugar, vanilla sugar if you have it (see **TIP**, page 182)*

4 eggs, separated

1 tablespoon vanilla extract

250g plain flour

2 teaspoons baking powder

a good pinch of salt

200ml pudding wine, such as muscat, or Noilly Prat Ambré if you have it

icing sugar for dusting, if you like

Preheat the oven to 170°C/150°C fan/gas 3. Lightly grease a 23cm springform baking tin and line the bottom with baking parchment. Butter the parchment.

Halve the plums along the seam and stone them. Toss them with the demerara sugar and line the tin with them, cut side down. Try to cram them as closely together as possible.

Beat together the butter and sugar until pale and light. Add the egg yolks one at a time, beating well after each addition. Beat in the vanilla.

In a separate bowl, whisk together the flour, baking powder and salt.

In another scrupulously clean bowl, whisk the egg whites until they form peaks.

Begin to add the wine and the flour mixture to the butter, sugar and eggs in alternate batches, starting and ending with some of the flour (flour/wine/flour/wine/flour), folding in well with a spatula after each addition. Fold in a third of the beaten egg whites with a spatula to lighten the batter. Then stir in the rest, lifting the batter with the spatula and gently folding it into the mixture. It should be well combined, but you want to keep in as much air as possible. Spoon the mixture over the top of the plums, smooth the top with a spatula, place the tin on a baking tray and bake in the oven for about 55 minutes, until a skewer or toothpick inserted into the middle of the cake comes out clean. Depending on your oven, it may take a little longer. Put it back into the oven and test every 5 minutes.

Place the cake tin on a cooling rack. Run a palette knife around the sides of the tin but leave it to cool for 15 minutes before releasing the sides of the tin and inverting it on to a plate. Gently remove the base of the tin and the baking parchment and dust the cake with icing sugar if you like.

TIP HOW TO MAKE VANILLA SUGAR

Put a few split vanilla pods into a jar with some caster sugar and seal. Leave for a couple of weeks for the flavour to develop. You can keep topping up the sugar, and I use recycled pods too – any pods I've used to infuse custards or sauces, I simply rinse and dry out, then add them to the sugar jar. My jar is probably twenty years old now and still going strong.

~

Chapter 14 ~ Cake will save you

Burnt honey and walnut cake

SERVES ~ 6–8

This is the perfect teatime cake just as it is. If you want to fancy it up, add the cream cheese icing. If not, just serve it with some crème fraîche or lightly whipped, gently sweetened cream.

FOR THE CAKE

60g raisins or sultanas

4 tablespoons Calvados, Armagnac, brandy or Earl Grey tea

200ml honey, plus an extra 2 tablespoons if you are going to make the icing

2 tablespoons lemon juice

250g walnuts

150g plain flour, plus a little more for preparing the tin

2 teaspoons baking powder

½ teaspoon salt

180g unsalted butter, room temperature, plus a little more for greasing the tin

4 tablespoons caster sugar

3 eggs, lightly beaten

2 teaspoons vanilla extract

FOR THE ICING, IF YOU'RE USING IT

180g cream cheese

2 tablespoons burnt honey (see main recipe) – reserve the 2 tablespoons before you mix the honey into the cake; warm very gently to make it liquid if at all stiff

½ teaspoon finely grated unwaxed lemon zest

Soak the raisins or the sultanas in the alcohol or tea for 4 hours. If you're in a hurry, just put them into a small pan with the liquid, bring it to the barest simmer, remove it from the heat and leave it to cool. Drain.

Put the honey into a small, heavy-bottomed pan and bring to a simmer. Cook for about 3 minutes – it will bubble up rather excitingly – until it becomes very fragrant and darkened slightly. Remove from the heat and stir in the lemon juice. Cool, then reserve 3 tablespoons of the honey to glaze the warm cake, and an extra 2 tablespoons if you are making the icing.

Preheat the oven to 180°C/160°C fan/gas 4. Butter a 23cm springform cake tin, dust it with flour, line the base with baking parchment and butter the parchment.

Scatter the walnuts on a baking tray and bake them for 8–9 minutes, until fragrant. Remove them from the oven (leave the oven on) and wrap them loosely in a clean tea towel. Let them cool for a couple of minutes, then rub them gently with the tea towel to remove some of the papery skin. You won't remove it all, but

removing some of it will reduce any tannic bitterness. Let them cool completely. Chop 50g of the walnuts coarsely, then put the rest into a food processor with a couple of tablespoons of the flour and pulse until very finely ground.

In a bowl, whisk together the rest of the flour with the baking powder, salt and the ground walnuts, then stir in the chopped walnuts. Toss the raisins in a couple of tablespoons of the flour mixture – this will help stop them all sinking to the bottom.

In a stand mixer or with a hand mixer, beat together the butter, sugar and cooled honey until very light and fluffy. Slowly add the eggs about a spoonful at a time, beating well after each addition; beat in the vanilla extract. Add the flour mixture about a third at a time, stirring and folding until just combined, then fold in the raisins. Spoon the mixture into the cake tin then bake for 35–40 minutes, checking after 25 minutes to see if it's browning too much on the top. If it is, cover lightly with foil. Bake until a toothpick comes out damp but with no crumbs clinging to it. Remove the cake from the oven and let it cool for 5 minutes before running a dinner knife around the edge and releasing it from the tin, then remove the baking parchment from the bottom and place it on a rack. Brush the reserved honey all over the top of the cake while it's still warm. It can become quite toffee-ish, so just warm it in a small pan or with a 10-second blast in the microwave. Leave it to cool completely, before adding the icing if you are using it.

To make the icing, lightly beat the cream cheese with the 2 tablespoons of reserved honey and lemon zest, then spread it over the top of the cake with a spatula.

The uniced cake will keep well in a tin for up to a week.

~

Chocolate and prune cake

SERVES ~ 6–8

When I'm in France, or in the mood for it, I sometimes use Noilly Prat Rouge instead of port to soak the prunes for this. Cocoa beans are one of the aromatics used in the sweet vermouth, so I find it works very well in many chocolate recipes.

FOR THE CAKE

300g prunes, stoned (sometimes it is easier to do this after you've soaked them, so if they resist a bit, wait until they have had their port bath)

about 200ml port or Noilly Prat Rouge, enough to cover the prunes in a bowl

some softened butter, for preparing the tin

40g cocoa, plus more for dusting the tin

200g dark chocolate, about 70 per cent cocoa, broken into small pieces

3 eggs, separated

100g light muscovado sugar

2 teaspoons vanilla extract

100g plain flour

2 teaspoons baking powder

¼ teaspoon salt

80ml milk

FOR THE GANACHE

100g dark chocolate, about 70 per cent cocoa, finely chopped

80ml double cream

Soak the prunes in the port for at least 4 hours or overnight. Drain them well, reserving the liquid. Take 100g of the stoned prunes and purée them with 2 tablespoons of the port until smooth, either with a stick blender, in a mini chopper or by passing them through a sieve – they won't be silky smooth, but near enough will do.

Preheat the oven to 180°C/160°C fan/gas 4. Lightly butter a 24cm springform cake tin and dust it lightly with cocoa. Tap it hard over the sink to get rid of any excess. Line the base of the tin with baking parchment and butter the parchment.

Put the chocolate into a heatproof bowl over a pan of barely simmering water – the bottom of the bowl should not touch the water – and melt the chocolate. Cool very slightly and mix with the puréed prunes, then cool completely.

In a stand mixer or with a hand mixer, beat the egg yolks with the sugar until light and fluffy. Whisk in the vanilla, then fold in the chocolate and prune mixture.

In a separate bowl, whisk together the flour, cocoa, baking powder and salt.

Arrange the prunes in the bottom of the prepared tin.

Chapter 14 ~ Cake will save you

Fold the flour and cocoa into the chocolate mixture until just combined, then stir in the milk and 2 tablespoons of the pruney port.

In a separate bowl, whisk together the egg whites until they form stiff peaks, being careful not to over-beat or they will become grainy. Add one third to the chocolate batter to loosen it, then gently fold in the rest with a spatula, retaining as much of the air as possible.

Spoon the cake mixture over the prunes and gently smooth the top. Bake for 35–40 minutes, until a toothpick inserted into the middle comes out clean. Cool in the tin for 20 minutes, then turn out on to a rack to cool completely.

To make the ganache, put the chocolate into a small, heatproof bowl. Heat the cream in a small saucepan until just steaming – don't let it boil. Pour the cream over the chocolate and leave for 5–8 minutes. Stir with a spatula until smooth and glossy, then immediately pour it over the cooled cake.

Serve with cream, crème fraîche or vanilla ice cream, either as they are or with a little of the pruney port stirred in or trickled over the top.

The cake will keep sealed in a tin for up to 3 days.

~

Blood orange seed cake

SERVES ~ 6–8

The dilemma is real. I love a good, plain cake with all my heart and soul, and yet I have an unquenchable desire to be fancy from time to time – my northern roots showing.

So here is my beloved seed cake recipe all gussied up with a blood orange drizzle. The blood orange season is so short I am always looking for new things to do with them to make the most of it, and that's how this recipe was born. The first time I made this cake, I was going to watch Arsenal women's football team play with my fellow food writers and Gooners Thane Prince and Signe Johansen, and this was my contribution to our Meadow Lane picnic. They liked it and I hope you will too, and PS You can make it with a non-fancy orange too if you want.

150g unsalted butter, room
temperature, plus a little more
for greasing the tin

100g caster sugar

50g light muscovado sugar

3 eggs, lightly beaten

200g self-raising flour

¼ teaspoon salt

4 tablespoons candied citrus peel,
diced, plus an additional long
strip for the top of the cake if you
like (see how to make your own,
page 195)

1 tablespoon caraway seeds

1 tablespoon Madeira*

1–2 tablespoons whole milk

FOR THE DRIZZLE
juice of 1 blood orange

1 tablespoon caster sugar

1 tablespoon Madeira*

*You can substitute sherry or Marsala for
the Madeira if you like, or leave it out.

Preheat the oven to 180°C/160°C fan/gas 4. Lightly butter a 21 × 11 × 6cm loaf tin, and line the bottom with buttered baking parchment. Or simply use a bought liner and get on with your life.

Cream together the butter and sugars until very light and fluffy, in a bowl with a wooden spoon or in a mixer with the K-shaped beater attachment or with a hand mixer. Add the eggs a little at a time, beating well after each addition and adding a bit of the flour if the mixture looks like it is going to curdle. In a separate bowl, whisk together the flour and salt, then gently fold into the butter mixture with a spatula until only just combined. Fold in the candied peel and caraway seeds. Add the Madeira and a little milk, just enough to give the batter a smooth, soft texture – it should drop easily from a spoon. Spoon it into the baking tin – place a long strip of peel on the top if you have one – and bake for 45 minutes, until a toothpick inserted in the middle comes out clean. If the cake begins to darken too much before it is fully cooked, drape a piece of foil over the top.

While the cake is cooking, make the drizzle. Put the juice into a small pan with the sugar and heat gently over a low heat until the sugar dissolves. Remove from the heat and add the Madeira.

Take the cake out of the oven and while it is still warm, skewer the top all over with holes. Immediately pour over the drizzle mixture. Allow to cool completely in the tin before turning out.

This cake keeps quite well sealed in a tin for a few days.

You can buy very good candied peel now (I love souschef.co.uk – they sell not just orange and lemon peels but the more chichi yuzu and bergamot by mail order), but if you eat and cook with as many oranges as I do, it's a shame not to make your own. The compost heap can only take so much peel. This also gives you the advantage of being able to put a big strip of peel on top of the cake just before you put it in the oven, which always looks beautiful and tastes so good once you've baked it.

To make your own candied peel, put large strips of raw peel into a pan and cover generously with cold water. Bring to the boil and simmer for 5 minutes. Drain and repeat, but this time simmer for 30 minutes, keeping an eye on it so that it does not boil dry and topping up with boiling water from the kettle if you need to. Put a sieve over a bowl and drain the peel, reserving the cooking water. Measure the cooking water and return it to a clean pan. Add 100g granulated sugar for every 100ml of cooking water so you have an equal amount of sugar and water, and heat gently, stirring until the sugar dissolves. Add the peel and simmer for 30 minutes or so until it is translucent and very soft. Remove the pan from the heat and leave the peel to cool in the syrup. Place a wire rack over a baking sheet and remove the strips of peel from the pan with tongs. Place them on the rack to dry out for an hour or so. Sprinkle some more sugar on a sheet of baking parchment and toss the peel in the sugar to coat. Leave them to dry out for 3 hours, or even overnight, then pack them into an airtight storage jar, where they will keep for about 6 weeks. I like to keep them in big pieces and chop them up as needed.

~

Chapter 15

How to cook on holiday

IT'S 3 A.M. AND WE'RE RATTLING ALONG, dashing for the 5.30 a.m. Euro-tunnel, half the ham sandwiches prepared for the journey consumed between our house in Stoke Newington and the Leyton roundabout, a distance of perhaps three miles, when I have that sickening heart thump of having forgotten something.

It wasn't the passports, or the train reservation, or the dog. I had sunscreen and mosquito spray, straw hats and espadrilles, new paperbacks and a fully-loaded Kindle, credit cards and a wallet full of Euros unspent on holidays past. No, what I was sure I had forgotten, the essential piece of luggage, was a tarte Tatin tin.

All the professional cooks and food stylists I know have their go bag: an essential bundle of kit which contains everything from surgically sharp knives to citrus presses, measuring spoons, rasp-like graters, pastry brushes, cherry stoners, tweezers and fish scalers, oyster knives and blowtorches, which means they can be out of the house and cooking on gas, or induction or whatever – often temperamental – source of heat they're expected to work with that day.

When it comes to self-catering holidays, keen cooks often need their own go bags. The truth is, you probably need more than you have but not as much as you might think. Many of us have had that frustration – arriving at a flat or cottage that looked so promising online, probably chosen for its local food producers, shops and markets, those same producers, shops and markets featuring heavily in the online pictures of this idyllic food haven . . . to find the kitchen tricked out with whatever useless tat the owner deemed too much trouble to lug to the charity shop. Blunt knives, wobbly chopping boards, pans and lids that never seem to have met each other, tin openers that are simultaneously blunt and slightly terrifying, bottle openers that make you light a candle at the altar of the god of screw caps . . . If you pick your holiday destinations as a sort of grown-up gastronomic Disneyland, hoping to excavate the soul of a region with a knife and fork, it's a bit crushing.

In her book *Summer Cooking*, Elizabeth David wrote, 'The kitchens of holiday houses, whether cramped and larderless, or vast, bare, with a day's march between sink and stove, usually have a stony bleakness in common. However adequate the beds or satisfactory the view, the kitchen equipment will probably consist of a tin frying pan, a chipped enamel saucepan, one Pyrex casserole without a lid, and a rusty knife with a loose handle.' This situation has improved a little in this era of competitive Airbnbing, but unfortunately not enough for those of us who are keen cooks to lower our guard. You never know when a chipped saucepan incident will arise to ruin your mood, though you could probably sell that saucepan to a food photography prop house for enough to cover a decent lunch out.

So I'm sharing with you here my holiday kitchen essentials. I hope you'll understand and won't laugh too much. Of course the full list depends on whether you're flying or driving. This is my full on-manoeuvres packing list for when I'm going to a place I haven't stayed in before. Pare your list down according to mood, baggage allowance and law.

- You need knives. A small paring knife and a larger cook's knife of about 20–30cm will see you through almost everything, and a decent vegetable peeler. If you're flying, these will obviously have to go in the hold.

- A small, sturdy chopping board, possibly wooden if you're keen on the 'gram.

- A pan big enough to cook pasta and mussels if that's your sort of thing. It's also good for making stock, if like me you can't even throw out a chicken carcase on holiday.

- A decent frying pan. You can also use this to make your tarte Tatin in (page 201).

- If you're a keen baker or an unsure cook, a small set of digital scales and some measuring spoons can be helpful.

- Then there are location- and season-specific things, depending on where you're going and what time of year it is – cherry stoners and oyster knives fall into this category. I've often thought I can do without a cherry stoner, but then I can never resist cherries, and after the first few kilos, I succumb to the desire to make a clafoutis or compote, and then I have to go out and buy a stoner. Please don't trouble me with the YouTuber's life hack of using a paperclip. First find your paperclip, for a start. And then the whole kitchen looks like there's been a bad murder and you've only stoned four cherries. Next, you've gone off the idea of the clafoutis and you possibly hate cherries now, and that can never be allowed to happen. This means I now own about five cherry stoners.

- Some helpful small things, such as a rubber spatula, a fine Microplane for grating citrus peel, garlic and ginger, a set of tongs.

- A salad spinner, because I love a leaf and soggy ones won't do. And yes, I do know about spinning them round in a tea towel. This might be good for toning your arms, but it never gets the leaves properly dry and there are seldom enough tea towels in rentals anyway (see below).

- I always take extra microfibre cloths and tea towels, as there are never enough in rental places. I take an apron because I'm a messy cook, and a good set of oven gloves because invariably the ones you find in rentals are made from tissue paper embroidered with some cutesy saying or a local landmark, and third-degree burns are a buzzkill.

- If I'm leaving the country, I also take a pair of the biggest Marigold washing-up gloves, as even the largest European size is too small for my sturdy peasant hands.

PS The tarte Tatin tin was there all along, hidden beneath the salad spinner and the moules pan.

Tarte Tatin, without the tin

SERVES ~ **6–8**

I like to use crisp eating apples for this, such as Granny Smiths. In France, I buy circles of puff pastry, which makes this a very quick and impressive tarte, or I make a simple pâté brisée if I have time and am in that sort of mood. In England, I buy a sheet of ready-made all-butter puff pastry and make it fit the best I can. The secret to a good tarte Tatin is to be brave while you caramelize the apples and to have a little courage when turning it out – once you've mastered these two issues you have a very impressive pudding, which is genuinely quite easy to make. You need a heavy-bottomed frying pan, ideally one with an ovenproof handle, but if you don't have one of those, just wrap the handle tightly in a couple of layers of foil. Of course, you may have a proper tarte Tatin tin. Brownie points for that.

1 × 325g sheet of all-butter puff pastry

a little flour, for rolling out

120g unsalted butter

200g caster sugar

2 tablespoons white wine vinegar or cider vinegar

about 800g crisp eating apples, such as Granny Smiths – about 6–7 of them – peeled, cored and quartered

TO SERVE

crème fraîche, thick cream, whipped cream or vanilla ice cream

Take your frying pan – I use a heavy one that's 25cm in diameter – and place it over the unrolled sheet of pastry. This will give you an idea as to how much you need to roll it out to make it fit the pan. You want the diameter of the pan, plus about 1cm all the way round to tuck in around the edges. And later on, you'll need a plate large enough to turn the tarte out on to, so seek that out now too.

Place the pastry between two sheets of baking parchment or cling film very lightly dusted with flour and roll it out to the right diameter using the pan as a template (the pan, plus 1cm all the way round), then cut it into a circle as neatly as you can. Transfer the pastry on the sheet of paper or cling film on to a baking sheet and use a fork to pierce it about 12 times all over – this will help the steam to escape and the pastry to become crisp in the oven. Refrigerate the pastry for an hour.

Melt the butter with the sugar in the frying pan over a medium heat, and let it cook for 5 minutes or so until it starts to lightly caramelize. It might look like it is crystallizing a bit before it caramelizes, but don't worry. It is very forgiving, so hold

your nerve – it will produce a lovely smooth caramel in the end. Add the vinegar – it'll bubble up a bit. Put the apples in the pan, cut side up, arranging them tightly together. Don't worry if the pan feels crowded; they will shrink a little as they cook. Turn the heat down a bit, put the lid on the pan and cook the apples, rattling the pan from time to time, for about 6–8 minutes, until the apples are softened and the caramel has turned a darker brown.

Remove the pan from the heat and let it sit for 5 minutes. Preheat the oven to 200°C/180°C fan/gas 6.

Arrange the disc of pastry over the top of the apples, tucking it in inside the edges of the pan. Slide the pan on to a baking sheet and place it in the oven. Bake it for 15 minutes, then lower the temperature to 180°C/160°C fan/gas 4 and cook for a further 15 minutes, until the pastry is beautifully golden. Let it sit for 5 minutes (no longer, as if it cools too much it's a nightmare to turn out, though see TIP below if you have problems). Cover the pan with the serving plate, then, using oven gloves or a couple of dry tea towels, swiftly invert the tarte on to the plate. If any of the apples stick in the pan, quickly lift them out and arrange them on the pastry – no one will ever know. Let the tarte cool for 10 minutes before serving, though it's also delicious served warm rather than hot, if you want a little leeway with lunch.

TIP
If you leave the pan for a little too long before turning out the tarte, gently warm it on the hob for a minute or two to loosen the caramel.

Chapter 16

~

Texan summers

PRACTICALLY THE FIRST MINUTE I ARRIVED at the University of
St Andrews in 1983, I met The Texan and fell instantly in love, in that
can't-breathe-can't-talk-can't-think way you do when you're barely eighteen.
He wore denim dungarees ('overalls', as he would say), plaid shirts and
cowboy boots entirely unironically. He'd spent the summer at drama
school and sailing a yacht around the Greek islands. Compared to the
well-scrubbed, tweed-jacketed specimens at Stanhope Young Farmers,
The Texan was dazzling. And I allowed myself to be dazzled. Often.

Over the next few years, I spent summers in Houston. We lived in the
downstairs flat of a house his dad owned near Rice University. We had lots
of parties. I cooked my way through the *Silver Palate Cookbook,* which I had
stolen from his stepmother's bookcase. It was quite new then, written by
Sheila Lukins and Julee Rosso, who ran a tiny gourmet food shop of the same
name on the Upper West Side in New York. Of course the recipes included
apple pies and oatmeal cookies, but also strange poetry – arugula, pesto, pasta
puttanesca, and their famous chicken Marbella, which I still make today. Our
tall larder fridge, twice the size of the one that had sustained me all through

my childhood in England, contained pots of homemade crème fraîche, raspberry vinaigrette and tarragon chicken salad, much to the amusement of The Texan's brother, who played football for the University of Texas and could consume a whole roast chicken with his bare hands as swiftly and graciously as saying good morning (they both had delicious manners).

During the day, I tended our little garden, attempting to dodge fire ants and mosquitoes and any other known and unknown insects out to devour my pale and tender flesh. In the evenings, I did my best not to sweat through my 80s shoulder pads in flashy, glittery, highly padded 1980s restaurants such as Tony's and Annie's Café. Either that, or we sought out some lot by a busy road where they served the best ribs, barbecue or Tex Mex food I'd ever tasted, possibly because I had never tasted any of them before and had precisely nothing to compare them with. It was exciting, intoxicating, hot. My whole life smelled of coriander and limes.

Because fighting off mosquitoes, going out to lunch and reading fat Judith Krantz paperbacks by the pool isn't apparently a full-time occupation, I got jobs at the Houston Symphony and a local architect's office, both of which I was entirely unqualified for but I got because of my *absolutely adorable* accent. I suspect that it was because of my *absolutely adorable* accent that they allowed me, the lowliest of staff members, to take Friday afternoons off if I wanted, to go to the ranch or the lake house that belonged to my belovèd's family, or to some debutante's party where they floated the pool with gardenias and called it a good time.

I liked these cheerful, friendly and wholesome girls, The Texan's friends since childhood. Untrammelled by performative seriousness, or the desire to read Voltaire in the original French, or to watch *Koyaanisqatsi* without nodding off or feeling the need to discuss Philip Glass's haunting score over pints of warm snakebite, they were sharp and funny and fun. We sat on the dock at the lake house and added rhinestone edges to jeans and painted T-shirts and drank frozen margaritas or bottles of icy Lone Star beer. In the evenings, we grilled steaks, or catfish we'd pulled out of the lake earlier. Days were hazy, humid, and nights were filled with stars. I was young and everything smelled of coriander and limes.

Chicken-fried steak: not as bad as it sounds

SERVES ~ 2–4

The Texan first cooked this for me in his little student flat in St Andrews, one cold, winter evening with the condensation running down the windows. It seemed an odd thing to do to a steak, especially on a student's budget, but in the land of the deep-fried Mars bar it felt churlish to mention it. Besides, I was blinded by love. And in fact – when served with mashed potato and gravy – it's so entirely comforting, whether blinded by love or not.

I like to trim the fat from the steaks and render it in the vegetable oil before I fry the meat to add even more flavour, but it's fine just to fry them in vegetable oil too.

The traditional white gravy is essentially a roux. I know it might sound mad to English ears, but it's quite delicious. Serve it with mashed potatoes and buttered green beans. Sometimes I make the chicken-fried steak on its own, without the gravy, and serve it with pickles. But please don't ever tell a Texan I do this.

2 sirloin steaks, about 200g each,
   fat trimmed off and reserved
   (see above)

salt and freshly ground black pepper

vegetable oil, for frying

FOR THE SEASONED FLOUR
150g plain flour

80g cornflour

1 teaspoon salt

1 teaspoon freshly ground black
   pepper

1 teaspoon cayenne pepper

½ teaspoon dried thyme

FOR THE BATTER
2 eggs, lightly beaten

50ml buttermilk

FOR THE WHITE GRAVY
300ml whole milk, warmed
   (but you don't need to do
   this until the steaks are cooked)

Preheat the oven to 120°C/100°C fan/gas ½. Line a baking tray with kitchen paper.

Trim the fat from the steaks, and reserve it if you are going to use it to add flavour to the vegetable oil. Place the steaks between two sheets of cling film and bash with a rolling pin or meat tenderizer until they are about 5mm thick. At this point I like to cut them in half, so I have four pieces about 12 × 10cm. Season them with salt and pepper.

In a shallow bowl, whisk together the flour, cornflour, salt, pepper, cayenne and thyme. In another bowl, whisk together the eggs and buttermilk.

Dip the steaks into the seasoned flour and give them a good shake, then into the egg mixture, then into the flour again – you want some nice craggy bits, because that is where the essential crunch is.

Warm about 1cm of oil in a large frying pan over a medium–high heat. If you like, add the trimmed beef fat and cook until it is golden – this will help add flavour. Remove the beef fat with tongs (at this point I scorch the roof of my mouth by eating the fat, and then get back to work). Again using the tongs, carefully lower the steaks into the pan – they will spit and generally be fairly badly behaved, so take care. You may need to cook them two at a time so you don't crowd the pan. Fry on one side for 3 minutes, then turn them over to fry for another 3 minutes, until the batter is crisp and golden brown. Use the tongs to lift them carefully into the prepared baking tray. Put them into the oven to keep warm while you fry the next batch and make the gravy.

Pour all but 2 tablespoons of the oil from the pan. Over a medium–low heat, sprinkle on 2 tablespoons of the remaining seasoned flour and stir for a couple of minutes until the flour starts to brown. Slowly pour in the warm milk, whisking all the time, and let it simmer gently until thickened, which should take 3–4 minutes – you want it quite thick. Season very well with salt and pepper. Serve with the steaks, in a warmed jug. I like to serve it on the side, so it doesn't diminish the crunchy coating.

~

Meemaw's margarita pie: just as good as it sounds

SERVES ~ 6–8

The Texan's grandparents lived in a ranch-style house in a suburb of Corpus Christi. We often visited them at weekends, to go to the beach, or just to hang out in their garden sipping sweet iced tea and telling stories. On those Friday nights, we left Houston after work and hammered down Highway 59 the 180 miles to Corpus, arriving after the grandparents had gone to bed. Meemaw usually left us something in the fridge. Once it was slices of this pie, with a note, 'A friend at church gave me this recipe. When I put the tequila in I just couldn't taste it so I kept adding a bit more and a bit more. Now I see when you let it sit a while, you can certainly taste it.' Reader, it will knock you on your ass. In a good way.

FOR THE PRETZEL CRUST
120g pretzels

3 digestive biscuits, about 50g

*120g unsalted butter, melted, plus a
little more for greasing the tin*

4 tablespoons caster sugar

FOR THE FILLING
*320ml double cream or whipping
cream*

5 juicy limes (see **TIP***)*

1 × 397g tin of condensed milk

75ml tequila

*1 tablespoon triple sec, Cointreau or
other orange liqueur*

salt

Preheat the oven to 180°C/160°C fan/gas 4. Lightly butter a 24cm loose-bottomed flan tin.

In a food processor, blitz the pretzels and biscuits into crumbs. If you don't have a food processor, put them into a plastic bag, seal well and bash with a rolling pin. Mix the crumbs with the melted butter and sugar and press them into the prepared tin. Use the bottom of a small tumbler to help you press it smoothly up the sides. You want it to be as even as possible, but don't stress out about it too much. Bake for 10 minutes, until lightly browned. Remove from the oven and cool completely.

Whisk the cream until it thickens and forms soft peaks. Measure 100g of the whipped cream into a bowl, cover and refrigerate. You'll use this to decorate the pie later.

Juice 4 of the limes (see TIP) – you want about 125ml of juice. Whisk it together with the condensed milk, tequila, triple sec and a good pinch of salt. Fold in one third of the remaining whipped cream, gently mixing it in with a rubber spatula until well blended. Then fold in the rest. Smooth the filling into the cooled shell.

Grate over the zest of one of the limes, with a Microplane grater ideally, being careful not to grate any of the white pith. Alternatively, pare the zest with a sharp vegetable peeler and cut it into thin strips.

Next, either pipe the reserved whipped cream into rosettes all around the edge of the pie – I rather like the retro look of this – or simply spoon it around the edges. Cut the remaining lime into very thin slices and arrange the slices on top of the tart.

Freeze the tart for at least 8 hours or overnight – you can make it a couple of days before you want to serve it if you like. Remove it from the freezer and leave it to sit for about 10 minutes before cutting into it.

TIP

If the limes aren't particularly juicy, giving them a 10-second blast in the microwave on full power should help.

~

Chapter 17

How living in Soviet Russia taught me to cook

IN 1990 AND 1991, I LIVED IN MOSCOW, on the seventh floor of a concrete block in Oktyabrskaya Ploshchad. Had our apartment been on the fashionable side of the building, we would have looked out on a towering bronze statue of Lenin, his coat flapping in the wind as he gazed sternly towards Gorky Park. As it was, we looked out on to a car park full of faded, boxy Ladas and shiny, boxy Volvos. At night, rats performed their own ravenous ballet in the open rubbish bins.

We had a full-time maid, Katya, and a driver, Uri. This sounds grand but in those days it was mandatory for foreigners. It was how, during the last, brittle glimmers of the Communist superpower, the authorities kept track of what we were doing, who we were seeing.

Each morning, I asked Katya, 'How's the weather?' In winter, she had a special glint in her eye. 'Oh, minus 25°C,' or, even better, 'Minus 30°C!' 'That's very cold,' I'd say, taking a quick, comforting slug of coffee. 'Oh, it's not so bad. It's just the way I like it!' she'd say, unpeeling coat, hat, scarf and gloves from her short, round body and changing her thick boots for dainty patent leather shoes. No wonder Napoleon and Hitler didn't stand a chance against these people.

Our flat had a sitting room, two small bedrooms, a kitchen and a bathroom. I could, with a little stretching, have dusted the whole place from the hallway. Not much for Katya to do. I was twenty-four years old, excited, a bit scared. I'd had a few Russian lessons from a long-lashed, razor-cheeked Serb called Zoran in a bedsit in Earl's Court before I left England. I'd just about mastered the Cyrillic alphabet and learned how to say zdrah-stvooy-tee. I remember thinking that it was hardly surprising a nation with such a long word for 'hello' had a reputation for being unfriendly.

So, Katya became my Russian teacher. We drank tea and talked. Sometimes we went out and talked. Sometimes we bought ice cream, even in winter, or hot beef pastries from vendors outside the Oktyabrskaya Metro station. She taught me how to use the underground and take a tram, how to pay in shops (see something in a cabinet and ask to look at it, ask the salesperson for a ticket, queue up at another counter to pay for it, go back to the first counter with your receipt and collect your purchase, which would then be carefully wrapped in brown paper. You better not be in a hurry). And, most importantly, she took me to the markets.

I loved the huge Centralny Rynok, the Central Market, best of all. While there might have been shortages elsewhere, and shops with empty shelves and long queues, this was a place of abundance for those of us with foreign incomes and access to hard currency. In the main hall, there were flower stalls selling chrysanthemums with creamy, billowy heads the size of turnips, and carnations dyed lurid shades of electric blue, stalls heaped with walnuts and raisins, strings of dried mushrooms, barrels full of pickled cabbages and cucumbers, boxes of perky lettuce, crates of potatoes and carrots, bunches of dill, coriander and parsley as big as a Cossack's fist, little bundles of thyme and bay, baskets of lemons and oranges. Citrus fruits were brought up from the southern republics in suitcases by gold-toothed sellers who took advantage of air fares fixed by the state years ago, so selling a few lemons was enough to pay for their 2,000-mile round trip between Tblisi and Moscow.

Behind the main hall, there were two long, low buildings. The one on the left sold meat, everything from rows of waxy piglets to legs of lamb, ribs of beef and enormous slabs of pork. In the white-tiled building on the right, stout women with white overalls buttoned tightly over their woollen coats sold milk, yoghurt, cream and cheese in old jam jars, and brown paper bags filled with eggs.

In London, I'd bought fruit and veg from the cheerful men on Berwick Street market, tiny, beautiful single-girl lamb cutlets from the butcher on Brewer Street, sardines from the fishmonger on Endell Street, garlicky slices of salami from I Camisa on Old Compton Street. When I left work late, or towards the end of the month when funds were running low, I'd pick up things for dinner at Sainsbury's on the Finchley Road. Neat. Clean. In Moscow, I was thrown into a world of grubby vegetables and strange cuts of meat sold by men in bloody aprons. Katya taught me to hunt down the best produce, negotiate the best prices. I enjoyed, for the first time in my life, a sense of the seasons passing. After a long winter and chilly spring, the first strawberries, tomatoes and green beans were more tempting than gold.

While we shopped, Uri leaned against our grey Volvo in his black leather jacket, smoking strong, filterless cigarettes and chatting with the other drivers. (As I sit here at my desk in Hackney thirty years later, I think of the smell of those cigarettes, mingled with dill, tangy brine from the vats of pickles and the sour milky fug from the dairy, and within a single breath I am in Moscow again.) As soon as Uri saw us, he would throw his cigarette to the ground to come and help us with our bags. He was short, but broad-shouldered and very strong. He had been a captain in the army and, to be honest, he probably still was. I remember once coming out of the market and seeing his face fall, a flicker of anger. Inside, I had bought some colourful string bags – the kind that are so eco-friendly fashionable now – and had decanted my shopping into them. 'No!' said Uri. 'Not these. These are for babushkas. You need plastic bags.' He made it very clear to me that I had made him lose face in front of the other drivers. Ideally, I should have a Harrod's bag, but an M&S bag would do at a pinch, something with western writing on it at least, but this granny bag was an abomination.

In a city where pensioners lived on 90 roubles a month, less than I'd pay for a leg of lamb, I learned not to waste a scrap. In my kitchen on the seventh floor, I cooked simply and often and threw lots of parties. There were few restaurants, so we often ate in each other's homes. I'd packed *Mediterranean Food* by Elizabeth David, I think because I imagined reading her sensual prose would see me through a bleak Russian winter. But I cooked from it, working my way through its pages, tumbling my Russian vegetables in her French dressing, turning fat little mushrooms into her champignons à la provençale and transforming those Georgian citrus into crème à l'orange. Julia Child said, 'You learn to cook so that you don't have to be a slave to recipes. You get what's in season and you know what to do with it.' Well, in those dark winter months, I had time, great ingredients, a warm kitchen, an eager audience and, importantly, Mrs David at my side, teaching me from her recipes how to cook without recipes.

I cooked for The Foreign Correspondent (TFC, not to be confused with the Turkish Food Centre on page 37) every day, often taking our dinner into his office because the three-hour time difference meant that he filed his copy late at night. Sometimes I made curries from the lamb I'd bought at the market, and this in particular horrified the Russian staff, who thought they smelled revolting and couldn't understand why we would willingly eat anything that burned your mouth and made your eyes water from the heat.

Because I knew no one but TFC when I arrived, I joined the International Women's Club. It held its first meeting of the season each September in Spaso House, the residence of the American Ambassador, an opportunity for members returning from summers in Cape Cod and Lagos and Île de Ré and other, generally better-catered corners of the globe to catch up over coffee and cakes, and to sign up for the various groups the club ran in everything from Russian poetry to cooking and yoga. A woman who lived in my building, a BBC reporter, told me to sign up for the architecture group. 'It's quite competitive to get in, and even more competitive when you're in. You take turns to lead walks with a dozen or so women about parts of the city. You get your patch and you have to research it, and try to get permission for you all to enter any special buildings on the route, and then give a talk to the rest of the women on what you've learned. It's genuinely more terrifying than anything I ever do at work, but it's the best way to learn the city.'

For the next year, every Friday morning I took the Metro to meet my architecture gang, mostly diplomatic wives, journalists' wives, the wives of men who were here to set up joint ventures as the country opened up. Wives, essentially, and most a lot older than me. It was certainly – along with the maid and the driver – like something from another age. But they were kind and they were funny and they were generous, and they took me under their wing as we stamped around the city with our thermoses of coffee and Tupperware containers of biscuits. The one rule of Architecture Club was that you always showed up for Architecture Club, even when the snow was thick on the ground and the thermostat hit minus 20°C. Those Art Nouveau mansions weren't going to look at themselves.

These women were my raft. They helped me find my feet, invited me to their lunches and dinners and embassy parties, and helped me throw parties of my own. By the next year, I'd set up my own group, an international cookery group where we met in each other's homes to cook a lunch from our own countries, because I have always known the shortest distance between two people is, 'Would you like something to eat?' My inaugural dish was Lancashire hotpot.

With Russian friends, we explored Moscow's Georgian restaurants, which generally served the best food in the city – the freshest and most interesting and usually the most likely to contain vegetables. Sometimes they came to our apartment. When I first arrived, this felt dangerous, risky for them, but then as time went on, it felt less so. There had been a shift. Not one huge thing, but many small things, imperceptible daily changes, and suddenly sitting in our tiny apartment and eating golubtsy might not get you tailed or harassed or arrested. Of course there were always risks, always a floor in every building inhabited by foreigners where the lift didn't stop, but I knew things were changing when I went down to tell the concierge that our heating wasn't working and she showed me into the room behind her little office. It was dominated by a board with all our flat numbers listed on it with small speakers underneath each number. Her cup of black tea steamed on the desk. She shrugged. I shrugged. So many things were breaking down, the chances of all the microphones in all our apartments working were slim. And what of it really? At the very most, she might have got out of it a Lancashire hotpot recipe, or one for a world-class apple pie, possibly coq au vin. Less Cold War, more hot dinner.

Beetroot in horseradish sour cream

SERVES ~ 2–4

On Sundays, we often went to U Pirosmani, a Georgian restaurant by the walls of the Novodevichy convent. Then, Georgian food was a revelation to me, though now I realize it has a lot in common with the Turkish food I love so much from my favourite Hackney *ocakbaşı* restaurants. Compared with the often grey, sometimes stodgy dishes we ate in Russian restaurants, Georgian food was colourful, fresh, spiked with herbs, citrus, nuts and salty cheese. I loved best the hot and cold *zakuski* at the beginning of the meal, the small salads and pickles, all served with still-warm bread. This beetroot salad is one I first made during that time and continue to make today.

60g walnuts

5 tablespoons sour cream

2 tablespoons Greek yoghurt

1 tablespoon horseradish sauce, or freshly grated horseradish for a spikier, punchier salad

½ teaspoon salt

a generous squeeze of lemon

4 medium-sized beetroot, about 500g total weight, roasted, peeled and cut into 2cm cubes (see **TIP** below)

small bunch of dill, tough stalks removed and roughly chopped

TO SERVE

slices of rye bread and butter

Preheat the oven to 180°C/160°C fan/gas 4. Scatter the walnuts on a baking sheet and roast for 6–8 minutes, until fragrant and lightly toasted. Cool and roughly chop.

In a bowl large enough to hold everything, whisk together the sour cream, yoghurt, horseradish, salt and lemon juice. Add the beetroot, walnuts and dill (save some of the walnuts and dill to scatter over the top). Turn everything over with a spatula until well combined but not totally blended – I think the slight raspberry-ripple effect is lovely and stops it looking like something you might buy from a garage chiller cabinet. Scatter the remaining dill and walnuts over the top just before serving, with rye bread and butter.

This salad will keep quite well in the fridge, sealed and ungarnished, for a couple of days.

TIP HOW TO ROAST BEETROOT

Of course, you can easily buy cooked beetroot but sometimes it's good to make your own so you can season them just how you like them. Don't peel

the beetroot yet, just give them a good scrub and place them in a roasting tin on a large sheet of tin foil. Trickle on some olive oil and sprinkle with sea salt, then rattle the tin until they are well coated. You can leave it at this if you want, or add some bay leaves, sprigs of thyme, a trickle of cider vinegar, and/ or a few garlic cloves, bashed just enough to break the skins, no need to peel them. Cover with foil and crimp together the edges with the foil lining the tin, to make a sealed packet (this cuts down on clean-up, which is always a good thing) and roast at 200°C/180°C fan/gas 6 for 45 minutes to an hour. You'll know they're done when you can pierce them easily with the blade of a small sharp knife. Cool slightly and then peel them. I do this by slicing off the root and the stem end then rubbing them vigorously with kitchen paper, like I'm drying a wet puppy. This is usually enough to bring off the skin without staining your hands too much, but if your hands do look like you just did a bad murder, rubbing them vigorously with the cut side of a lemon or raw potato will usually get the worst off.

~

Golubtsy

SERVES ~ 4–6

Versions of these cabbage rolls exist all over Russia, the Ukraine, Poland and Slovakia, filled with combinations of meat, grains, vegetables and herbs. You can certainly use this recipe as a template to create your own, juggling the filling to suit your own taste and what you have in the cupboard and fridge. The name 'golubtsy' means 'little pigeon', which I suppose – if you squint a bit – is what they look like all nestled cosily in the dish.

12 large leaves from a Savoy cabbage,
*   or more if your cabbage is smaller*

130ml sour cream

FOR THE SAUCE
40g unsalted butter

1 bay leaf

1 medium onion, about 170g, diced

salt and freshly ground black pepper

2 cloves of garlic, halved, green germ
*   removed, and very finely chopped*

—›

¼ teaspoon caraway seeds

1 tablespoon concentrated tomato
    purée

1 × 400g tin of chopped tomatoes

1 tablespoon red wine vinegar

FOR THE FILLING

25g unsalted butter, plus a little more
    for buttering the dish

1 medium onion, about 170g, diced

2 cloves of garlic, halved, green germ
    removed, and very finely chopped

500g pork, coarsely minced

150g cooked pearled spelt, rice or
    barley

1 egg, lightly beaten

a handful of fresh parsley, tough stalks
    removed, and fine stalks and leaves
    chopped – about 20g finished
    weight

3 tablespoons chopped fresh dill, plus
    some more whole fronds to finish

1½ teaspoons salt

1 teaspoon freshly ground black
    pepper

First, make the sauce. In a heavy-bottomed saucepan over a medium–low heat, warm the butter with the bay leaf. When the butter is melted, add the onion and a good pinch of salt and sauté gently, stirring from time to time, until softened and translucent, about 15 minutes. (If you want to speed things up, you can sauté the onions for the filling in a separate pan at the same time.) Add the garlic and caraway seeds and sauté for a further minute. Add the tomato purée and stir for a minute or two. Add the tomatoes and vinegar, season with salt and pepper, and simmer gently for 30 minutes while you get on with the rest.

Prepare the cabbage leaves by trimming the stems and shaving down the thick part of the stalk with a vegetable peeler (you need to be able to fold them easily when cooked). Fill a bowl with iced water and bring a pan of salted water to the boil. Blanch the leaves for 2 minutes, then pick them out with tongs and plunge them into the iced water. Pat them dry with a clean tea towel or kitchen paper. Add a couple of ladles of the cabbage water to the tomato sauce.

To make the filling, melt the butter in a heavy-bottomed saucepan over a low heat, then add the onion and a good pinch of salt and sauté gently, stirring from time to time, until softened and translucent, about 15 minutes. Add the garlic, sauté for a minute, then tip into a bowl and cool.

Preheat the oven to 180°C/160°C fan/gas 4.

Put the pork, cooked spelt, egg and herbs into the bowl of cooled onion and garlic, season very generously with salt and pepper and mix together well – I like to do this with my hands. If you would like to check the seasoning, break a little bit off, fry it, let it cool a bit, then taste it – add more seasoning as necessary.

Divide the meat mixture between the cabbage leaves. Place a spoonful in the centre of each cabbage leaf, tuck in the sides and roll up as neatly as you can from

the stalk end. Lightly butter an ovenproof dish or casserole and arrange the rolls seam side down in it. Pour over the sauce – it won't feel like enough, but that's fine. You don't want it to be soupy. Spoon the sour cream over the top and bake for 40–45 minutes, until the sauce is bubbling and thickened. Scatter over some dill fronds and serve straight away.

TIP

You can make this up to the point just before you dot on the sour cream, cover it and refrigerate for a day if you want to make it ahead, or freeze it with the sour cream on for up to a month.

~

Lamb plov

SERVES ~ 8–10

Plov, pilaf, pilau, pulow, wherever they come from, these dishes all feature some combination of rice, meat, vegetables, and often dried fruit or sometimes nuts. In her book *Red Sands*, my friend Caroline Eden has a delicious plov recipe, which includes fresh quince. Plov is a very important dish in Uzbeki culture, traditionally cooked by men, and with as many variations as there are families who serve it. I know versions of it kept me going through many cold Moscow days. Also, I just like saying 'plov'.

To go alongside it, assemble a platter of tomatoes, chopped cucumbers and lots of fresh, green herbs, such as parsley, coriander and mint.

500g basmati or Arborio rice

3–4 tablespoons sunflower oil or rapeseed oil

1kg lamb shoulder, cut into 3cm cubes – this is about 1.7kg on the bone

salt and freshly ground black pepper

1½ tablespoons cumin seeds

½ teaspoon chilli flakes

¼ teaspoon cayenne pepper

5–6 medium onions, about 1 kg, halved and cut into thin slices

1 bay leaf

1 tablespoon pomegranate molasses

120g raisins

$\rightarrow$

4 tablespoons barberries, about 20g
  (available from Middle Eastern
  stores)

a generous pinch of saffron

1 whole, unpeeled garlic bulb

400g carrots, cut into chunky batons,
  about 5 × 2cm

a small handful of chopped fresh
  parsley

a small handful of pomegranate seeds

Soak the rice in a bowl of cold water for 30 minutes, then drain and rinse very well, until the water runs clear.

In a large, lidded, heavy-bottomed casserole (I use my largest Le Creuset casserole – 29cm and 4.7-litre capacity), warm 2–3 tablespoons of oil over a medium–high heat. Season the lamb with salt and pepper and brown each cube well – you'll need to do this in batches so that you sear rather than steam the meat (see TIP below). Put the browned meat on a plate as each piece is cooked. Once you've browned the meat, lower the temperature and add the cumin, chilli flakes and cayenne and stir for 30 seconds. Next, toss in the onions and bay leaf. Add more oil if you need to, though you probably won't, as the lamb will have rendered its fat. Sauté, stirring from time to time, until the onions are softened and golden, about 20 minutes. Return the meat to the pan with any of the juices which have accumulated on the plate. Pour over just enough boiling water from the kettle to cover and stir in the pomegranate molasses, raisins, barberries and saffron. Place the whole garlic bulb in the middle of the pan. Simmer on a very low heat, partially covered, until the meat is very tender, about an hour and a half. Taste and add more salt and pepper if necessary. Add the carrots and simmer for 5 minutes with the lid on.

Spread the rice in a layer over the top of the meat, doing your best not to stir it in. You want it just sitting on top. Sprinkle on a little salt. Carefully add more boiling water from the kettle, just enough to submerge the rice by 2cm. Put the lid on the pan and simmer very, very gently until the rice is tender, about 25 minutes. Remove from the heat, lift the lid and quickly make about half a dozen holes in the rice with the handle of a wooden spoon so that the steam can escape. Replace the lid and leave for 15 minutes, before removing the garlic bulb and carefully turning the plov out on to a large serving plate. Place the garlic bulb on top and sprinkle over the parsley and the pomegranate seeds. Let people help themselves, taking a garlic clove or two to squeeze into the sauce or on to some bread.

TIP HOW TO BROWN MEAT

When browning meat for a stew or casserole, you want to get it really brown – that's how you get great depth of flavour. The secret to this is not to crowd the pan, so the meat doesn't sweat, which means that you'll often have to brown it in batches. Don't move it around too much and don't worry if it sticks. Once it's properly browned and has formed a crust, it should move very easily.

~

Martina's Circassian chicken

SERVES ~ around 6, even more if served with other dishes

My neighbours on the seventh floor of the building on Oktyabrskaya Plochad were a Turkish diplomat and his German wife, Martina. I spent many afternoons sitting on her carpet playing with their baby, Yasmin, and chatting to Martina, who was funny, clever, charming, the perfect diplomatic wife, and who seemed to take all the challenges of our peculiar situation in her graceful, athletic stride. She entertained a lot. We all entertained a lot. When she made a buffet, it always included this chicken dish. If you can't get hold of Aleppo pepper, use a mixture of half-and-half chilli flakes and paprika. This is very good as part of a buffet, or as a simple lunch with a green salad (see page 27). Any leftovers are delicious wrapped in a flatbread too. It is quite rich, so it goes quite a long way.

50g unsalted butter

1 medium onion, about 70g, finely diced

salt and freshly ground black pepper

FOR THE POACHED CHICKEN

1 small chicken, about 1.4kg

1 small onion, about 120g, quartered

1 carrot, roughly chopped

2 celery sticks, roughly chopped

1 bouquet garni, comprising a few fresh parsley stalks, a thyme sprig and a bay leaf tied together with kitchen string

1 teaspoon salt

1 teaspoon coriander seeds

5 black peppercorns

4 allspice berries

3 cloves

FOR THE WALNUT SAUCE

150g walnuts

40g fresh white breadcrumbs

2 cloves of garlic, halved and green germ removed

1½ teaspoons Aleppo pepper (sometimes labelled pul biber)

250ml chicken stock (from poaching the chicken)

TO FINISH

30g unsalted butter

½ teaspoon Aleppo pepper (sometimes labelled pul biber)

30g walnuts, toasted (see **TIP**, page 258) and roughly chopped

a handful of fresh coriander leaves, roughly chopped

First, poach the chicken. Put all the ingredients into a heavy-bottomed saucepan into which the chicken fits fairly snugly and pour in just enough water to almost

cover the chicken. Bring to a gentle simmer and poach, covered, for 50 minutes to 1 hour, until tender (you'll know when it is done as the leg will pull away easily). When the chicken is cool enough to handle, carefully remove it from the pan, remove and discard the skin, then use two forks to shred the meat into bite-size pieces. Strain the stock into a clean pan and simmer hard for 20 minutes until reduced a little (you need at least 400ml). Taste and season with salt and pepper.

In a large frying pan or saucepan, melt the butter over a medium heat and add the onion with a good pinch of salt. Sauté, stirring, until they begin to turn golden, about 10–15 minutes, then add the shredded chicken and 200ml of the reduced stock. Cook, stirring occasionally, until the liquid has almost evaporated. Remove from the heat.

In a pestle and mortar, pound together the walnuts, breadcrumbs, garlic and Aleppo pepper into a rough paste, and then gradually work in the other 200ml of stock. Alternatively you can whiz this together in a food processor or with a stick blender, but be careful not to let it get too smooth. Taste and season with salt and pepper.

Toss the chicken together with the walnut sauce, turn it out on to a serving platter and shape it as best you can into a slightly pointed dome (this is the way I was taught to serve it, and it looks a little nicer than just a mound). Warm the butter in a small frying pan over a medium heat until it starts to smell slightly nutty, sprinkle in the Aleppo pepper, sauté for 10 seconds, then trickle it over the chicken. Sprinkle on the chopped walnuts and the coriander and serve, just warm or at room temperature.

VARIATION

You can finish the chicken with a trickle of walnut oil and a sprinkling of chopped fresh parsley in place of the melted butter and coriander if you like.

~

Ginger, cardamom and lemon pryaniki

MAKES ~ **16 pryaniki**

Every Friday morning, sun, sleet, or snow (often snow, so often snow), I went on guided walks around Moscow with my ladies' architecture group. We each of us brought something: thermoses of hot chocolate, little cakes, folk remedies for frostbite. I sometimes took these biscuits, which may not win any beauty contests but don't dismiss them because they are poor, obscure, plain and little. They are absolutely delicious and the best friend a cup of tea ever had.

160ml runny honey

50g butter

1 teaspoon cider vinegar

1 teaspoon ground ginger

1 teaspoon ground cardamom

½ teaspoon ground cinnamon

¼ teaspoon ground allspice

¼ teaspoon freshly grated nutmeg

a couple of grinds of black pepper

200g plain flour, or a mixture of
    150g plain flour and 50g rye flour

½ teaspoon bicarbonate of soda

½ teaspoon salt

finely grated zest of 1 unwaxed
    lemon, grated directly over the flour

1 egg, lightly beaten

60g stem ginger, drained and finely
    diced

FOR THE GLAZE

120g icing sugar

3 tablespoons fresh lemon juice,
    passed through a tea strainer or
    fine sieve

In a small pan, gently warm the honey and butter with the vinegar, spices and black pepper, just until the butter has melted, then let it cool.

Whisk together the flour/s, bicarbonate of soda and salt in a bowl. Grate the lemon zest over the top, being careful not to go down to the bitter white pith, and stir it in. Beat in the honey mixture and the egg until smooth – it will be a sticky dough. Fold in the stem ginger. Cover the bowl and refrigerate for at least an hour, or overnight (the flavours will get stronger). Keeping the dough chilled until the last minute also makes the pryaniki easier to roll out.

Preheat the oven to 180°C/160°C fan/gas 4. Line a large baking sheet or a couple of smaller ones with non-stick baking parchment or Silpat. Roll the dough into balls the size of a large walnut – they should be about 30g each – and place them on the sheet, about 4cm apart. Bake for 13–15 minutes, until just golden. While they're in the oven, make the glaze – whisk together the lemon juice and icing sugar until

smooth, then, while the pryaniki are still warm, dip them into the glaze, turning them over with a fork, and place them on a wire rack to cool completely.

VARIATION
Use about 40g chopped crystallized lemon or orange peel (see page 195) in place of the stem ginger.

~

Chapter 18

I never met a baguette
I didn't like

EVER SINCE I WAS EIGHT YEARS OLD and sitting in Mrs Snow's (Madame la Neige, *s'il vous plaît*) French class for the first time, I have been enraptured by all things French, from the Sun King and Madame de Pompadour to Johnny Hallyday and Françoise Hardy. As a teenager, I bobbed my hair, wore red lipstick, read *Paris Match*, and generally slunk about the place like County Durham's very own Simone de Beauvoir. I stopped short of a beret, but only just. I certainly wore one in my head, if not on it.

My first proper trip to France was on a school exchange. I stayed with a family in the small town of Villeneuve-sur-Lot for three weeks. I was thirteen and I loved everything indiscriminately. Every day, I volunteered to go and get the bread from the bakery and nibbled the end of the crust on the way home. I bought stacks of Clairefontaine exercise books with their neatly lined pages and attempted to write my 'r's in that distinctively French way. I loved my host's 2CV with the Communist Party sticker in the back window. I even loved the weekly folk-dancing classes in the local *salle des fêtes*.

But most of all I loved the food and the everyday rhythm of family life, which revolved around meals, the making of them, the acquiring of the components of them, the discussion of them and then, *enfin*, the eating of them. I enjoyed the gentle hum of chat in the square, terracotta-tiled kitchen as dinner was being made. Laure and Jerôme – my hosts' children – and I set the table, taking plates, linen napkins (on a school night), cutlery and glasses from the wooden dresser to lay on the round, oilcloth-covered table. Sometimes I would get to make the salad dressing – a high honour – whisking together red wine vinegar, mustard and olive oil into a thick emulsion in a small glass. Once or twice I got to wash lettuce, trim green beans or help make the all-in-one flourless chocolate cake which appeared on the table every Saturday.

At home in England, meals were something to be got out of the way as efficiently as possible, to fettle and move on, in order to race more efficiently at life. So the slow intensity of French life was intoxicating.

I went back several times to stay with this family. Once, the grandmother invited us all to lunch on Easter Sunday. A pan of water already boiling on the stove, she went out to cut asparagus from the bed by the kitchen door. It took five minutes from living to cooked and on a plate. I dipped each spear into a little bowl of vinaigrette and attempted to eat it as elegantly as possible. So far, so simple. The next course was pigeon. Whole pigeon. Head on, in every sense. One on each plate, nestled on a bed of wilted spinach, their dull eyes and sharp yellow beaks facing each diner in what can only be described as an accusatory manner. I did then what I still do now when faced with something unfamiliar: I watch everyone else and just get on with it as best I can. Even when it came to the tiny spoon by each plate which was intended to scoop out the brains.

Of course it is mandatory if a little unfashionable these days to mention Elizabeth David at this point. Her imperious tone jars with today's taste for chummy, everything-in-fifteen-minutes-or-less recipes. Bish, bash, bosh. But my mother – who knew nothing about cooking but everything about words – bought me her books, an acknowledgement that though she was entirely indifferent to food and cooking, she honoured my serious interest in it even if she didn't understand it. And of course, I loved the books. I still love them.

At home today, even now, a lot of the cooking I cleave to is simple, with a slight French accent. Sometimes the French is silent. It's more about the shopping, seeking out really good ingredients, and ease, than the pungent zip of tarragon or the aniseedy warmth of chervil in every bite. Sometimes it's more explicit. I mean, my poule au pot might as well be flying a tricolour.

Today, I spend each summer in a confident Languedocian village on the shore of the Étang de Thau, where oysters are literally cheap as chips, Picpoul de Pinet is the local wine and Noilly Prat vermouth is made just on the other side of the narrow harbour. My weeks there follow a familiar rhythm of applied nothing. I know the market days of villages and towns within a twenty-kilometre radius. I know who to go to for mussels or for a gigot d'agneau, and who sells the best tomatoes or peaches. Each morning, the smell of scorched flour draws me to Les Saveurs d'Eugène, the village's best bakery, for baguettes and croissants. To avoid the intense heat of the day, I walk the dogs in soft, pink light as the sun comes up over the lagoon, and in the evening, through the narrow *ruelles* of the village, sometimes stopping off at Le Cochon Gourmand for some cheese for dinner, or the Bar Marine for an apéro. I can truly do what comes naturally to me, which is plan one meal, or several meals, while eating another. The food I make here, in the house on the edge of the water, is seasoned with this sense of summer ease that I try to bring to my cooking all year round, whatever the season and wherever I find myself. So *merci*, Madame la Neige, *merci* for everything.

Marseillanais cocktail (you need it)

SERVES ~ 1

I love a simple cocktail with an edge of bitterness to it and this couldn't be simpler or more delicious, with a bowl of salted almonds or olives Sétoises (see below).

2 parts Noilly Prat Dry
1 part Noilly Prat Rouge
ice, lemon, orange

Put 2 or 3 large ice cubes in a rocks glass, pour over the Noilly Prat Dry and the Noilly Prat Rouge, give it a stir and garnish with a twist of lemon and a twist of orange.

~

Olives Sétoises

SERVES ~ 4–6, with drink

Sometimes you're offered these with your apéritif in French bars and restaurants, but more usually you see them on the olive stalls you find in every single market. Silky, punchy aïoli, the ketchup of the South of France (except on those less chi-chi occasions when ketchup actually is the ketchup of the South of France), and salty olives are a great combination. You want crisp, meaty green olives such as Lucques to counterbalance the richness of the aïoli. If you like, add a bit of heat and colour with piment d'Espelette (see page 254), paprika or even a dab of harissa. They're very good with a Marseillanais cocktail (see above). You will need to serve them with cocktail sticks, because of the divine messiness.

a couple of handfuls of green olives,
  such as Lucques

FOR THE AÏOLI

2–3 garlic cloves, peeled, halved, green
  germ removed

a good pinch of fine salt

2 egg yolks, room temperature

200ml oil – I like a third olive oil,
  two-thirds sunflower oil

a squeeze of lemon juice

OPTIONAL

a pinch of piment d'Espelette, paprika
  or a dab of harissa

I'll give you instructions for making aïoli in a pestle and mortar, which is what the purists like, but I almost always make it with my mini food processor, possibly my most used piece of kitchen kit. First, make sure everything is at room temperature – oil, eggs, everything. If you are making the aïoli in a bowl, it helps if you warm it slightly first – just fill it with hot water, tip the water out and dry it well.

Soak a clean dishcloth and wring it out. Place it on the counter and put your bowl or mortar on top – this will ensure it doesn't move about.

Pound the garlic and salt into a paste with the pestle and mortar, or if you're using a bowl, chop it together into a paste on a board, then put it into the bowl. Add the egg yolks and stir until well blended. Begin to add the oil a drop at a time, stirring constantly, either with a pestle or a whisk. To be absolutely correct, always stir in the same direction. As it thickens you can begin to add the oil slightly more quickly, but don't overdo it or it will split and all your hard work will be for nothing (*BUT* see below if it does). When you've incorporated the oil, taste and add more salt if it needs it, a squeeze of lemon and any of the other seasonings if you fancy them. If it's too thick, thin it with a little hot water.

If you're using a mini food processor (this is too small a quantity to make in a large one), still chop the garlic into a paste by hand first, then put it into the machine and whiz until blended with the egg yolks. Then, with the motor running, proceed as above. The aïoli will keep in a jar in the fridge for a couple of days – cover the surface with cling film so it doesn't develop a skin.

Toss the olives in just enough aïoli to coat and serve immediately.

TIPS **IF YOUR AÏOLI SPLITS . . .**

All is not lost. In a clean bowl, whisk up another egg yolk and begin to add the split mixture a drop at a time, beating constantly, and you should be able to rescue it.

This makes too much aïoli to dress a few olives for the cocktail hour, so here are a few more things you can do with it . . .

Serve it with crudités, all kinds of seafood and fish, dot it on to the moules farcies (see page 248), drop a spoonful into fish soup, serve it with croquetas or fat chips, or of course make lots and create a Grand Aïoli, but that's a whole 'nother story.

~

Huîtres gratinées

SERVES ~ 4, as a starter

Each summer when we arrive in Marseillan, one of the first things we do is walk around to the other side of the harbour to have these oysters at the Château du Port, a restaurant that looks like a château rather than a château that has become a restaurant. The village is on the Étang de Thau, a huge lagoon separated from the Mediterranean by a thin cordon of sand and filled with over 700 wooden oyster tables – you can see them from the air when you fly into Béziers airport, a pleasingly orderly grid – from which they cultivate more than 13,000 tonnes of briny bivalves each year. In the markets and shops along the edge of the water, they're almost literally as cheap as chips and we eat them raw all summer long, so sometimes for a change I like to cook them too, particularly the larger ones, which can be a bit much when raw to be quite honest. This is a great recipe – inspired by one made at the Château – for those nervous about eating raw oysters. And for the cook, it's an impressive starter – you can prep it all an hour or so before you want to serve it and simply assemble everything and put it under the grill just before you sit down. And oh yes, it contains Noilly Prat vermouth, the village's other famous export, which matures in oak barrels under the sunshine only a shell's throw from the restaurant.

a few handfuls of rock salt

1 dozen oysters, shucked, juices reserved (see **TIP** *below)*

20g unsalted butter

200g spinach, well washed, with the water still clinging to it

2 tablespoons Noilly Prat Dry, or other dry vermouth

1 small shallot, roughly chopped

1 sprig of fresh tarragon

3 tablespoons crème fraîche

40g finely grated Gruyère or Comté cheese

TO SERVE

a baguette, or other good bread

Place the rock salt on a baking tray (it needs to be the right size to fit under your grill) in 12 small mounds with little hollows in the middle.

Open the oysters (see below), making sure you reserve all the briny liquid. Rest the bowl-shaped parts of the shells in the little divots of rock salt; discard the flat parts of the shells.

Warm the butter in a frying pan over a medium heat, add the spinach and cook just until wilted. Divide between the oyster shells.

Put the juices reserved from shelling the oysters into a small pan with the vermouth, shallot and tarragon and simmer together for a minute. Drop the oysters into the pan and poach for 20 seconds, then fish them out with a slotted spoon and place one in each shell on top of the spinach.

Put the grill on to heat up as high as it will go.

Add the crème fraîche to the pan with the juices and simmer until thickened – you want the consistency of double cream. Strain into a bowl, then spoon a little of the mixture over each oyster. Sprinkle some cheese on each one and carefully place the tray under the grill for just a minute, until the top is golden and bubbling. Serve right away, with good bread to mop up the delicious, creamy sauce.

TIPS

I use the rock salt to steady the shells on the baking sheet – I keep a jar of it for just this purpose and use it again and again, for oysters, scallops, any shell that needs steadying.

HOW TO SHUCK AN OYSTER

I could waste 500 words telling you how to shuck an oyster and we would both run the risk of nodding off. There are thousands of brilliant tutorials on YouTube and it's much better to watch someone who really knows what they're doing if you want to learn – and you probably should, it's a life skill up there with knowing how to change a tyre or put up a shelf. Buy a decent oyster knife with a guard on it – they're not expensive – and possibly a protective oyster glove if you are as clumsy as me, and take your time.

Tielle Sétoise

At the end of the nineteenth century, Italian fishermen from Gaeta, north of Naples, arrived in Sète with their families, their boats and this recipe for octopus pie, which they in turn learned from the Spanish. Made from a sturdy yeasted dough, it was robust enough to last for several days at sea – it reminds me a little of Cornish pasties, where the pastry is as much packaging as nourishment. It was poor people's food, and the Italians managed to keep it to themselves. Italian children were embarrassed to take tielles with them to school, wishing they had croissants like their French classmates. But in the 1930s a French woman from nearby Agde, Adrienne Pages, married into the Italian community of Sète and set up a shellfish stall called La Reine des Mers, selling these special pies. Today, you find them all over the coastal towns and villages of the Hérault, and there are fiercely fought competitions each year as to who makes the best one.

Their distinctive red colour comes from the tomato sauce seeping through and staining the pastry. They were traditionally cooked in a terracotta dish called a *teglia*, from which their name is derived, but I use an ordinary tart tin and so does almost everyone else. Incidentally, if you are there and shopping for octopus, you may find them called *lou pouffe* in the Sétoise dialect, instead of the French, *le poulpe*.

about 1.2kg octopus – get your fishmonger to clean it or see the TIP, page 246

1 carrot, peeled and cut into big chunks

1 stick of celery, trimmed and cut into big chunks

1 bouquet garni, comprising 1 bay leaf, a generous sprig of fresh thyme and a few fresh parsley stalks tied together with kitchen string

2 teaspoons salt

6 black peppercorns

FOR THE SAUCE

3 tablespoons olive oil, plus a little more for brushing the top

2 medium onions, diced, about 320g

2 bay leaves

a few sprigs of fresh thyme

salt and freshly ground black pepper

5–6 fat cloves of garlic, halved, green germ removed, and diced

3 tablespoons concentrated tomato purée

250ml white wine

$\longrightarrow$

1 × 400g tin of chopped tomatoes

350ml passata

2 tablespoons red wine vinegar

120g black olives, stoned

1–2 teaspoons piment d'Espelette (see page 254), or sweet paprika

a good pinch of powdered saffron, or saffron threads

a small bunch of fresh parsley, about 15g, tough stalks removed (use them for the bouquet garni), leaves and fine stalks chopped

FOR THE DOUGH

400g plain flour

10g instant yeast, or 20g fresh yeast

a pinch of caster sugar

160–200ml warm water

1 teaspoon salt

4 tablespoons olive oil, plus a little more for brushing the tin and the dough

1 tablespoon concentrated tomato purée, plus a little extra for brushing the dough

First, cook the octopus. Place it in a large saucepan with the carrot, celery, bouquet garni and enough water to cover by 10cm. Add the salt and peppercorns and bring it to a simmer. Cook for 1½–2 hours, until the octopus is very tender when pierced in the thickest part with a knife. Let it cool in the liquid, then strain, reserving about 250ml of the liquid. Discard the vegetables and bouquet garni. Chop up the whole octopus with a knife – or, in the preferred way I have seen locals prepare it, snip it into bite-size pieces with scissors. At this point, you can cover the octopus and keep it in the fridge for a couple of days if you want.

Next, make the sauce. Warm the oil in a large saucepan over a medium–low heat, add the onions, bay leaves and thyme and a good pinch of salt and sauté the onions, stirring from time to time, until they're soft and translucent, about 20 minutes. Add the garlic and sauté for a couple of minutes, stirring, then raise the heat a bit and add the tomato purée. Cook it for a couple of minutes, until it loses its bright red colour, then pour in the wine and let it bubble away for a few minutes. Add the reserved cooking water from the octopus, the tinned tomatoes, passata, vinegar, olives, 1 teaspoon of piment d'Espelette or paprika, the saffron and some salt and pepper. Lower the temperature and simmer gently, stirring from time to time, until the sauce is a rich, red colour. Taste, add more piment d'Espelette if you would like it a little hotter, and more salt and pepper if it needs it. Add the octopus and simmer gently for a further hour. Remove from the heat, stir in the parsley, and cool.

While the sauce is cooking, make the dough. Mix a few tablespoons of the flour with the yeast, sugar and 60ml of the warm water in a small bowl. Cover and leave in a warm place for 30 minutes. Put the rest of the flour into a large bowl, whisk in the salt, make a well in the middle, then add the yeast mixture, olive oil, tomato purée and about 100ml of the water. Mix thoroughly, then turn it out on to a floured surface and knead it for a few minutes until smooth – it may need a further sprinkling of water. Put the dough into a lightly oiled bowl, cover and leave in a warm place until doubled in size.

Preheat the oven to 200°C/ 180°C fan/gas 4 and put a baking tray in the oven to heat up. Divide the dough into two pieces, one slightly larger than the other. Brush a 24cm tart tin with olive oil. On a floured surface, roll out the largest piece of dough and line the tin. Spoon in the filling. Roll out the second piece of dough a little more thinly than the first and lay it over the top. Gently press the surface, especially around the edge of the tin, to push out any air. Roll your rolling pin over the top to remove the excess pastry, or trim it with a knife. Now comes the magic part – to create the traditional crenellated edge (though if you can't be bothered, you can certainly just crimp it as you normally would). Start by making 1cm cuts in the edge of the dough, about 1cm apart, all the way around the pie. Fold over every second tab on to the top of the pie and pinch it down lightly to seal. Continue all the way around the pie, folding over every other tab. Make some holes in the top of the pie with a fork to help the air escape and to allow the red filling to seep through the top. Brush the top with the olive oil whisked with the tomato purée.

Place the pie on the hot baking sheet and bake for 30–35 minutes, until the pastry is crisp and golden and some of the juices are bubbling through the surface, staining the pastry a rich red.

Serve warm or cold, with a green salad.

TIP **HOW TO CLEAN AN OCTOPUS**

- Lay it firmly on a chopping board and make a straight cut just below the eyes.
- There's no delightful way of saying this, but scoop the organs out from inside the head and tug away any membranes. Next, take out the eyes with a sharp paring knife. The worst is over.
- Spread the tentacles out and look for the small hole in the middle. This is the beak, which has a sort of fingernail-ish texture. Use the paring knife to remove it.
- Rinse everything under running water, paying close attention to the suckers, which can be filled with grit and sand.

~

Moules farcies

SERVES ~ 6

This is a special dish, a celebratory dish, something for when you really want to push the boat out – which is to say it takes a little time, but most of it is taken up with opening the mussels and that really isn't too onerous once you get the knack (there is also a cheat's way, if you really can't stand it – see below – gleaned from Caroline Conran's joyous book *Sud de France: The Food and Cooking of Languedoc*). It's something to do while sitting down with a play on the radio or a podcast or an audio book. This is the kind of cooking I love – you look busy, but you're not doing much. It's also a very companionable recipe to make with a friend, sitting side by side at the kitchen table, dissecting scandal, working through your thoughts.

Stuffed mussels are served at restaurants all around the Étang de Thau, and when you taste them you'll understand why. The flesh of the mussel folds around the garlicky pork in a sort of meatball of dreams, and the shells help to flavour the rich tomato sauce (tomatoes, again, with no apologies).

2kg mussels, cleaned (see **TIP**, page 251)

150ml brandy or pastis

FOR THE SAUCE

3 tablespoons olive oil

1 large onion, about 220g, diced

1 bay leaf

½ teaspoon salt

150g lardons, cut into small dice

4 fat cloves of garlic, peeled, halved, green germ removed, and very finely chopped

4 tablespoons concentrated tomato purée

250ml red or white wine

600ml passata

1 × 400g tin of chopped tomatoes

2 tablespoons red wine vinegar

¼ teaspoon saffron powder or a pinch of saffron strands

a bouquet garni, comprising a few fresh parsley stalks, a sprig of thyme and a bay leaf tied up with kitchen string

½ teaspoon freshly ground black pepper

FOR THE STUFFING

110g fresh white breadcrumbs

150ml whole milk

600g coarsely minced pork, or a mixture of pork and veal

2 eggs, lightly beaten

2 fat cloves of garlic, peeled, halved, green germ removed, and very finely chopped

small bunch of fresh parsley, about 15g, tough stalks removed (use them in the bouquet garni), and chopped

salt and freshly ground black pepper

→

aïoli (see page 241) (optional)

rice or baguette, to soak up the sauce

First, get the sauce on. The longer it cooks, the better it will be. Warm the olive oil in a heavy-bottomed saucepan over a medium–low heat, add the onion, bay leaf and a good pinch of salt and sauté, stirring from time to time, until softened and translucent, about 20 minutes. Raise the heat a little and toss in the lardons. Fry for a couple of minutes, then add the garlic and cook for a minute. Stir in the tomato purée, combining it vigorously with the rest, and cook until it almost catches on the bottom of the pan. Stir in the wine and let it bubble for a couple of minutes before pouring in the passata, chopped tomatoes, red wine vinegar and saffron. Add the bouquet garni, salt and pepper, then reduce the heat and simmer very gently for at least an hour, possibly two, stirring from time to time, until the sauce has lost its redness and taken on a deep, rusty colour.

While the sauce is cooking, prepare the mussels. You need to open them up. Brace yourself, but it's honestly going to be fine. Slide a small, sharp knife into the long arc of the mussel shell, slide it around towards the hinge, then force it open flat like a book, with the two sides still attached. If you just can't be bothered with the faff, use Caroline Conran's excellent quick method. Pour a glass of white wine into a large pan, bring to the boil, throw in a couple of handfuls of the mussels, put the lid on and cook for 1 minute just until the shells begin to open. Fish them out with a slotted spoon, bring the liquid back to the boil and repeat until you've opened all the mussels. Strain the liquid and add it to the sauce. Prise all the shells open so they lie flat, like an open book.

For the stuffing, soak the breadcrumbs in the milk for 10 minutes to fatten them up, then drain off any excess milk. In a large bowl, mix together the bread-crumbs, minced pork, eggs, garlic and parsley and season well with salt and pepper.

Place an open shell in your hand, grab a small piece of the meat mixture and add it to the open shell – enough to slightly overfill it. Squeeze the shell closed and run your finger along the edge to remove any excess meat. Continue with all the shells. As you fill them, arrange them on their sides on the bottom of a large, lidded casserole dish in concentric circles, pushing them up snugly against one another and forming several layers. Very correct cooks tie them up individually with string so they can't open up while cooking, but nobody has time for that. I say that knowing that you have been reading this recipe for half of your natural life.

You may have slightly too many mussels or too much filling – just scatter any remaining mussels or stuffing over the top.

Place the casserole containing the mussels over a medium–low heat. Warm the brandy or pastis in a small pan, carefully light it and pour it over the mussels. When the flame subsides, pour over the sauce. To ensure the top layer of mussels doesn't open up, you can put a heavy plate or smaller pan lid over the top if you want, but I don't really mind if the meat drifts into the sauce. Cover and simmer very gently for 1 hour.

If you're using the aïoli, whisk a tablespoon of the sauce from the mussels into a few tablespoons of it to create a beautiful rouille.

Spoon the mussels into warmed bowls, over some rice if you like. Dot the rouille over the top if you are using it and serve immediately.

TIP **HOW TO CLEAN MUSSELS**

- Place them in a colander and rinse them well. Give open ones a sharp tap on the kitchen counter – if they're alive, they'll close up again. Discard any that don't close or are badly chipped.
- Tug hard at any beards to remove them. Cut off any stubborn ones with a knife, and slide the back of the knife against any barnacles if you are punctilious about getting rid of them (I am not).
- Next, scrub the shells clean with a stiff brush or wire wool pad and rinse again. They will keep in the fridge covered with a damp cloth for a day but are best cooked as soon as possible.

~

Macaronade Sétoise

SERVES ~ **6–8**

This rich and delicious stew is famous in Sète, where many families and restaurants have their own recipes, slightly tweaked and fiercely defended. I always think of Sète as the glittering town across the *étang* from Marseillan. It's the big city to us, population 42,000, scruffy, lively and glamorous, with its wonderful Wednesday market which snakes through the town's streets. At markets all over the region, you find stalls selling vats of macaronade, alongside stuffed squid and moules farcies (see page 248), and it is a *boucher-traiteur* staple too. I think I probably sampled them all in my selfless search to create this recipe.

Macaronade – a rich meat stew mixed with pasta – hints at Sète's historic Italian community. The brageole – thin slices of beef, seasoned with garlic and parsley and rolled up – derive from Italian *braciole*, often cooked with meatballs and Italian sausage in a tomato sauce.

Don't be put off by the length of this recipe. It's all very straightforward, and requires no particular skills. Traditionally, the Sétois enjoy it for Sunday lunch, but it really is perfect whenever you want a rich, soul-pleasing dinner for a cold day. It doubles and triples up beautifully too, so it is a very good and popular dinner for a crowd – you can do all of it ahead, just cook the pasta at the last minute and stir it into the dish five to ten minutes before serving. Though historically it was served with macaroni – hence the name – it seems the Sétois now prefer penne rigate, and so do I.

YOU WILL NEED . . . *Some wooden toothpicks or kitchen string.*

FOR THE BRAGEOLE

a big bunch of fresh parsley, tough stalks removed, leaves and fine stalks chopped, about 35g in total

5 cloves of garlic, halved, green germ removed, and very finely chopped

200g minced pork

1 teaspoon salt

½ teaspoon freshly ground black pepper

6 slices of beef – chuck, fillet or topside, about 100g each, as thin as possible

FOR THE REST OF THE MACARONADE

4 tablespoons olive oil

500g pork shoulder, cut into 3cm cubes

500g garlicky sausages, such as Toulouse sausages, or fresh Italian fennel sausages

→

2 onions, diced, plus one small, whole,
    peeled onion

2 bay leaves

2 tablespoons concentrated tomato
    purée

200ml full-bodied red wine

600ml passata

3 tablespoons red wine vinegar

3 whole cloves

1 teaspoon piment d'Espelette (see
    page 254), or ½ teaspoon paprika
    or cayenne pepper

salt and freshly ground black pepper

TO SERVE

600g penne rigate, or large macaroni

a mixture of grated Parmesan and
    Gruyère cheese, for scattering over
    the top

First, make the brageole. In a small bowl, mix together the parsley and garlic until
well combined. In a second bowl, season the minced pork with the salt and pepper
and mix it all in well – I do this with my hands. Lay out the pieces of steak – you
can use a rolling pin to make them flatter and thinner if you want (what a shame
that presence of a rolling pin in life often has the opposite effect on people) and
divide the parsley and garlic mixture between them, spreading it out in a thin layer.
Divide the pork between the beef, making a thin sausage about 1cm from the short
end, then rolling up fairly gently. Secure with one or two cocktail sticks or string.
If they are quite large, I often cut them in half. For speed, you can mix the parsley,
garlic, salt and pepper in with the minced pork, but I like the bright green layer.

In a large, heavy-bottomed saucepan, warm 2 tablespoons of the oil over a
medium–high heat and cook the brageole until they are gently browned all over –
the toothpicks make this a bit of a challenge, but do your best. Add more oil if you
need to. Remove them from the pan and set aside. Season the pork with salt and
pepper and brown in batches in the same pan (see TIP, page 228); set aside with
the brageole. Brown the sausages and – you know the drill – set aside. Add a little
more oil to the pan, lower the heat to medium–low, tip in the diced onions with a
good pinch of salt and the bay leaves and sauté them gently, stirring from time to
time until softened and lightly golden, about 20–30 minutes. Add the tomato purée
and stir for a couple of minutes, then pour in the wine and simmer for 4–5 minutes
before adding the passata and vinegar. Stud the small, whole onion with the cloves
and add it (traditionally, the Sétois add a clove for each serving, but that is a little
too Happy Christmas for me), along with the piment d'Espelette or cayenne and
some salt and pepper – go a little easy at this point on the s+p, as all the meat
has strong flavour.

Simmer gently for 20 minutes, then add the brageole, pork and sausages.
Give everything a good stir, bring to a gentle simmer, and cook, partially covered,
for about 2 hours, stirring from time to time. At this point you can cover it

completely and cook it in a 150°C/130°C fan/gas 2 oven for 2 hours if it's more convenient. You'll know when it is done because the meat will be very tender and the sauce will be a deep russet – if it's not, if it still looks red, keep going. You're almost there. Taste and add more salt and pepper if necessary. You can make it up to this stage a couple of days ahead, and refrigerate. Bring it to a gentle simmer before adding the cooked pasta.

Bring a large pan of water to a vigorous boil and salt well (see TIP below). When the water returns to a rolling boil, add the pasta and cook according to the package instructions, minus a couple of minutes (it will continue to cook in the sauce). Drain well, stir into the meaty sauce and cook for a further 5 minutes or so.

Serve with the grated cheese sprinkled over the top. I sometimes tip this into a gratin dish, scatter the cheese on top and put it under a hot grill until it bubbles up, because there are few things I love more than molten cheese.

This is the bit where I say serve with a green salad, for health. But only if you want to. I am not your mum.

TIPS HOW TO COOK PASTA

To cook pasta properly, you need more water and salt than you probably think you do. For perfection, I follow the guidance of the late, bracingly correct Marcella Hazan, who in her excellent book *The Essentials of Classic Italian Cooking* had this to say about salting pasta water: 'For every pound of pasta, put in no less than 1½ tablespoons of salt, more if the sauce is very mild and undersalted. Add the salt when the water comes to a boil. Wait until the water returns to a full, rolling boil before putting in the pasta.' So for most pastas, allow a minimum of 1½ tablespoons per 450g. Know this: undersalting is one of the unkindest things you can do to your pasta. Salting it properly elevates the simplest dish to joyful heights.

PIMENT D'ESPELETTE

This gently warming chilli pepper has been grown in and around the French Basque town of Espelette since the sixteenth century. It is mild – only around 1,500–2,500 on the Scoville scale, compared to cayenne's punchy 30,000–50,000. It can be used wherever you want to add a little spicy warmth – certainly some cooks in this part of France use it interchangeably with pepper. Try it with eggs, in mayonnaise or vinaigrettes, to season the Basque favourite piperade, or on fish or meat for the barbecue. You can find it in some delis, or by mail order from the wonderful souschef.co.uk.

WHY YOU DON'T NEED A GARLIC PRESS

All but the freshest, juiciest, youngest garlic often has a green shoot, the germ, in the middle of it, which can give a musty, bitter taste. You need to take it out, particularly if you are going to use the garlic raw in dressings, but I am in the habit of removing it for cooked dishes too. By the time you've got out a chopping board, peeled the clove, halved it and removed the germ, you might as well chop it by hand. And the washing-up is so much simpler.

~

Rustic pear galette

SERVES ~ 6–8

In the summer of 2020, during the height of Covid, we had to delay our trip to Marseillan and forgo the delights of peaches and melons, which in high summer I devour greedily, to the point of almost permanent stickiness. When we finally got there that September, every market and grocery stall was filled with beautiful Comice and Anjou pears and intensely sweet and dark Stanley plums, the kind they often save to turn into prunes. Almost every week after market day, I made a simple galette like this one. When you make yours, eat it warm from the oven with cream or ice cream, or at room temperature, with a scoop of crème fraîche.

FOR THE PASTRY

250g plain flour

¼ teaspoon salt

150g very cold unsalted butter, cut into small cubes

2 tablespoons light muscovado sugar

1 egg yolk

1 teaspoon vanilla extract

1 teaspoon cider vinegar

2–4 tablespoons iced water

FOR THE FILLING

3 firm pears, such as Comice or Anjou

juice and zest of ½ an unwaxed lemon (see recipe – grate the zest directly on to the pears)

20g toasted hazelnuts, coarsely chopped (see **TIP**, page 258)

2 tablespoons light muscovado sugar

20g room temperature butter

OPTIONAL

50g golden raisins

60ml Calvados or brandy

FOR THE HAZELNUT CREAM

30g finely ground toasted hazelnuts (see **TIP**, page 258)

1 egg white (use the yolk for the egg wash)

2 tablespoons icing sugar

1 tablespoon melted butter

½ teaspoon vanilla extract

FOR THE EGG WASH

1 egg yolk, whisked with 1 tablespoon cream or milk

1 tablespoon granulated sugar

If you want to use the raisins, put them into a bowl with the Calvados or brandy and leave them to macerate for a few hours. If you're in a hurry, cover with cling film and microwave them on full power for 20 seconds to speed up the process, or put them into a very small pan, bring to the barest of simmers, remove from the heat and leave to cool.

In a bowl, whisk the flour with the salt and rub in the butter with your fingertips until the mixture resembles coarse breadcrumbs with a few pea-sized pieces of butter still in it. Stir in the sugar. In a small bowl or cup, whisk together the egg, vanilla and vinegar. Make a well in the flour and pour in the egg mixture, then work it into the flour with a dinner knife until it comes together – you may need a little of the water, but go easy, a bit sprinkled over the top at a time, just enough to bring it together. Turn it out on to a sheet of cling film. Gently form it into a disc, wrap it well and refrigerate for an hour.

Place the pastry between two sheets of baking parchment lightly dusted with flour and roll it out to a circle of approximately 32cm. Place it, in its parchment, on a baking sheet and return to the fridge for 15 minutes.

Preheat the oven to 170°C/150°C fan/gas 3½.

Peel the pears, cut in half and remove the core, then cut each half into three or four slices, depending on the size of the pears. Place them in a bowl, grate the lemon zest directly over them, being careful not to grate in any white pith, and add the lemon juice. Toss to coat. If you're using the raisins, drain them and fold them gently in with the pears.

In a small bowl, whisk together all the ingredients for the hazelnut cream. Remove the top layer of baking parchment from the pastry. Spoon the cream on to the centre of the pastry disc, leaving a border of about 5–6cm around the edge. Arrange the pears on top of the cream, with the raisins scattered among them, then sprinkle on the chopped hazelnuts, the muscovado sugar and dot with the butter. Gently fold the pastry border up around the fruit, using the baking parchment to help you lift the pastry up and over. Don't worry if it tears a bit, just cobble it together as best you can – it adds to the rustic charm. Brush the pastry border with the egg wash and sprinkle on the granulated sugar. Bake for 45–50 minutes, until the pastry is golden and the fruit bubbling. Serve hot or room temperature.

VARIATIONS

Try this with apples, apricots or peaches too. If you are in a tearing hurry and just want something sweet for dinner, just make the pastry base, scatter some ground nuts mixed with a little sugar on to it to help soak up the fruit's juices, then heap on the fruit mixed with a little sugar and bake.

TIP TO TOAST NUTS

- Preheat the oven to 180°C/160°C fan/gas 4. Scatter the nuts on a lipped baking tray (with a flat sheet, you run the risk of them rolling off, never to be seen again). After 5 minutes, take the sheet out and stir.

- Return to the oven and check every 3 minutes. Use a timer. You will forget, until the inevitable scorching smell reminds you. Most nuts take no longer than 10–12 minutes. For almonds and hazelnuts with the skins on, you want the skins to be quite blistered. Remove from the oven and tip the nuts out on to a plate immediately to stop them cooking.
- If you are skinning walnuts, almonds or hazelnuts, tip them into a clean tea towel, gently fold over the edges and leave them to steam for 5 minutes or so. Then rub them vigorously in the tea towel to remove the skins – it doesn't matter if a few patches remain.
- You can grind nuts with a pestle and mortar or by pulsing in a food processor until you have the texture you want. Wait for them to cool before you chop them or they will turn into paste.

~

Chapter 19

Falling off the edge

WHENEVER WE GO TO WEST CORK AND WE GO INTO A PUB – which is one
of the very best things to do in West Cork – I am always losing my husband
in the crowd. This is not because he's sneaky or small; he's neither of those
things. It's because he suddenly looks like everyone else. If not everyone
else, then a good half dozen or so blokes at the bar. If my husband, Séan
Donnellan, ever goes into a witness protection programme, or is on the
run, or simply tires of greeting his adoring fans along the length of Stoke
Newington Church Street, this is where we will come to hide. Tell no one.

We spent our honeymoon on what Séan calls 'the crinkly edge tour'. We
began at the Hibernian Hotel in Dublin and then drove our way clockwise
around the coast, through Wicklow, Wexford and Waterford, Cork, Kerry
and Clare, Galway and Mayo, until we reached Sligo and Delphi Lodge
(see How to survive having people to stay, page 115). It was November and
it rained a lot but we didn't care. We stayed in faded old country houses
and a pub with walls pockmarked with bullet holes by the Black and Tans.
We lived, as far as I can remember, on oysters, brown bread and Guinness.
In Youghal, a woman in a shop already decked out for Christmas gave us

a nativity set when she found out we were on our honeymoon. I pull it out of its crinkled paper every year and think of her kindness, and wonder why I didn't try the same schtick in the jewellers' next door.

We go to Ireland as often as we can. Sometimes we bring our friends. In early 2020, just before the world went mad, we spent ten days in a cottage on the River Ilen with our friend Fi. It had a wooden kitchen which made you feel you were in the galley of a boat, an enormous fireplace which took up the whole of one wall, a spaniel that ran down the hill to visit from time to time, and donkeys in the field. We read and cooked and walked as close to the edge of Ireland as we could get.

Being enormously culturally sensitive, Fi and I went big on the concept of three different kinds of potatoes with every meal. Which is why, late one afternoon, we got Séan to drop us off at the supermarket in our nearest market town to buy potatoes. He stayed in the car to listen to the cricket* while we went into the shop.

We scored some spuds and then, as we walked past his magnificent chiller cabinet, we caught the eye of The Fishmonger. 'Can I interest you in these beautiful scallops, ladies? Fresh as they can be, from Dunmanus Bay this morning.' He certainly could. After a minute or two's chat, he said, 'You have to meet The Cheesemonger, but he's gone home, I'll call him.' Within minutes, The Cheesemonger strolled back in and about a minute after that, we were trying slices of Gubbeen, Durrus and some local Cheddar. Then – somehow – we were racking up half a dozen shots of local gin to try and then some poitín appeared from below the counter in a Stone's Ginger Wine bottle. By now, The Fishmonger had gone off to find us a cookbook with his favourite recipe for the scallops and we were being introduced to other shoppers and oh god, I think we were taking selfies. We worked out, The Cheesemonger, The Fishmonger and I, that we had an Irish food writer friend in common, so suddenly we were all texting her at her home in France to alert her, whether she liked it or not, to this happy coincidence.

The Fishmonger gave us a bag for life from the supermarket to pile our bounty into. He explained it was a status symbol the world over because it made people think you had a house in West Cork. Fi and I are now obviously ruined for Waitrose. Somehow we struggle on, and I use my bag for life all the time, hoping someone, anyone, will notice and give me the West Cork nod.

*Sleep, same thing.

Crab salad sandwiches

SERVES ~ 2

One very cold February a couple of years ago, we took a trip to West Cork with our friend Fi. On the fifth, for Séan's birthday, we drove out to Crookhaven, where you feel like the next stop is America because really, it is. We went to O'Sullivans bar and had birthday crab sandwiches and pints of Murphy's. Who needs candles and balloons?

That evening, as the wind howled outside the cottage and the River Ilen lapped closer and closer to the door, we lit the fire and lay on the sofas listening to the West Cork podcast about the still unsolved murder of Sophie Toscan du Plantier, a few days before Christmas in 1996. When it got to the part where it said the last place Ms Plantier was seen alive was O'Sullivans in Crookhaven, we all shrieked and leapt up from where we were sitting.

100g brown crab meat*

½ teaspoon Dijon mustard

½ teaspoon concentrated tomato purée

3–5 drops of Tabasco, or to taste

100g white crab meat

1 tablespoon mayonnaise

5–6 leaves of fresh tarragon, plus a few small leaves to finish

a few gratings of lemon zest – grate it directly on to the crab, using the small-hole side of a box grater or a Microplane grater

freshly ground black pepper

3 little gem leaves, finely shredded

a squeeze of lemon juice

2 slices of soda bread (see page 268 for Johann's soda bread), or good brown bread

a little unsalted butter, room temperature

TO SERVE

lemon wedges and a few small sprigs of fresh tarragon

In a small bowl, mix together the brown crab, mustard, tomato purée and Tabasco.

In another small bowl, lightly fork together the white crab with the mayonnaise and the tarragon, and grate the lemon zest over the top. Don't overmix it. Season to taste with a little pepper.

Toss the shredded little gem in a squeeze of lemon juice.

Butter the bread lightly. Spread on the brown crab meat, put some of the lettuce on top, then spoon on the white crab. Finish with some small sprigs of tarragon and serve with lemon wedges.

*Sometimes I cook the crab myself, but more often I buy prepared crab from the fishmonger, which means these entirely spoiling and delicious sandwiches are the work of minutes.

~

Egg sandwiches for the beach

SERVES ~ 4–6

I like to use a bought, French-style mayonnaise for these. It has a little mustard
in it, which I like, and has more character to it than Hellman's or other American-
style mayonnaises (not that I am knocking them, they have their place, see, for
example, my favourite potato salad, page 65), but do just use whatever you prefer.
For 'something green, chopped up', I use either rocket, watercress or chives, though
I often hanker for classic egg-and-cress and wonder why I don't grow cress on
blotting paper on a sunny windowsill as I did when I was a kid. It makes me a little
sad that we live in an age when cress is almost as difficult to find as blotting paper.

   If you're the kind of family who has a cooked rasher or two of bacon left
over from breakfast, chop that up finely and stir it in too. We're not, so sometimes
I cook a couple especially to mix in with the egg. A slim, finely chopped spring
onion is also a good addition.

5 hard-boiled eggs, roughly chopped

a generous spoonful or two of mayonnaise

something green, chopped up (see above)

salt and freshly ground black pepper

bread, slices or soft rolls

OPTIONAL

*a couple of cooked rashers of bacon,
   finely chopped; a spring onion,
   finely chopped*

Gently stir together the eggs, mayonnaise, green thing of choice, bacon and/or
spring onion if you're using them, and season well with salt and pepper. Spoon the
salad on to white bread or brown, slices or rolls. Do everything within your power
to avoid sand.

~

Johann's soda bread

One cold Sunday in February, Irish wine writer and restaurant reviewer Tom Doorley invited Séan and me and our friend Fi to lunch at his house in what he calls 'unfashionable East Cork'. I met Tom years ago on a press trip to Australia. We almost died in a calamitous dawn hot-air balloon escapade and then sorely disappointed the PR woman running the trip by refusing to climb the Sydney Harbour Bridge that afternoon, as that was quite enough of heights for us in one day thank you very much. On such things are friendships formed. So we went for a splendid lunch, and Tom's wife Johann made us the most delicious soda bread, which we ate with a lot of Irish butter and cheese. I simply couldn't have been happier. This is Johann's recipe, only very slightly tinkered with by me. I added a little black treacle, for richness, and a scattering of oats on the top for wholesome glamour, but neither are necessary. It takes minutes to stir together and is a great recipe for when there is no bread in the house and you need toast fairly urgently.

a little butter for greasing the tin
350g fine-ground wholemeal flour
60g pinhead oatmeal
1½ teaspoons salt
1 teaspoon bicarbonate of soda

1 tablespoon black treacle (optional)
540ml buttermilk (see **TIP***)*
2 tablespoons jumbo oats, for sprinkling on the top (optional)

Preheat the oven to 220°C/200°C fan/gas 7. Grease a 1kg loaf tin with butter. The one I use is 23.5 × 13.5 × 7cm.

Tip the flour, oatmeal, salt and bicarbonate of soda into a bowl and give everything a good whisk. Stir the treacle in with the buttermilk if you are using it (brushing the bowl of the spoon with a little cooking oil will make it a lot easier to measure the tricky treacle). Make a well in the centre of the flour and oats, then pour in the buttermilk. Stir it all together to make a soft mixture, a little like wet cement. Spoon it into the tin and bake for 40 minutes. When it's done, it should pop out when you attempt to twist the tin and sound hollow when rapped on the bottom. Or test by pushing a skewer or small sharp knife into the centre of the loaf, leave it for a moment, then pull it out. If it is clean and not sticky, the loaf is cooked. If the skewer is sticky, give the loaf another 5–10 minutes and test again. Leave the loaf sitting across the top of the tin to cool.

TIP
Johann says, 'If you can't get buttermilk for the recipe, 3 tablespoons of natural yoghurt mixed with 1 tablespoon of lemon juice and enough water to make up the volume works fine.'

~

Meringues for Queen Sophia

SERVES ~ **10**

At that same Sunday lunch at Tom and Johann's, we ended our meal with this spectacular pudding. As you might imagine, we drank several excellent bottles over several excellent courses, and it's testament to how wonderful this is that I remember it at all. It is a sort of Eton Mess-y concoction of cream and coffee meringues and while there are several stages, none of them are hard and you can do all of them imperfectly and still end up with the most impressive result. If the meringues are wobbly, you are bashing them up anyway, same with the praline, and if you can't be bothered to make the caramel, just buy a nice jar of dulce de leche and crack on. You can also make all the components the day before and just assemble them on the day (remember to leave enough chilling time, for you and the pudding, though). Oh, and I have no idea who Queen Sophia is, but she obviously had quite the life.

120g raisins – if you can get your hands on Muscat raisins, all the better

150ml Pedro Ximénez sherry

1 × 400g tin of condensed milk, or a jar of dulce de leche

a little vegetable oil

120g walnuts

120g caster sugar

1 litre double cream

FOR THE COFFEE MERINGUES

3 egg whites

a pinch of salt

180g golden caster sugar

1 tablespoon coffee extract, or 2 tablespoons good espresso powder mixed with 1 tablespoon boiling water

Put the raisins into a small bowl with the sherry, cover and leave to soak while you make the other components.

Next, make the meringues. Make sure the bowl and whisk are scrupulously clean – any trace of grease will prevent the egg whites from whipping properly. Line a baking sheet with non-stick baking parchment or Silpat and preheat the oven to 150°C/130°C fan/gas 2. Beat the egg whites with the salt until stiff, starting slowly then building up the speed, then begin beating in the sugar a spoonful at a time until you have used half of it. Once you've added half of it, you can add the sugar more quickly, and whisk until the meringue mixture is beautifully glossy

and stands in stiff peaks when you lift out the beater. Whisk in the coffee extract. Spoon on to the prepared sheet in 8 generous dollops. Put the meringues in the oven and immediately lower the temperature to 120°C/100°C fan/gas 1. Bake for 1½ hours, until you can lift the meringues off the paper or Silpat easily. Turn off the heat and leave the meringues in the oven until they are completely cool.

To make the caramel, put the tin of condensed milk on its side in a pan and add enough water to cover the tin by about 5cm. Bring to the boil and simmer for an hour, topping up with boiling water from the kettle if it needs it – be very careful not to let it boil dry. Remove from the heat and let it cool in the pan.

To make the walnut praline, first line a baking sheet with non-stick baking parchment or Silpat lightly brushed with vegetable oil. Scatter the walnuts on the parchment. Tip the sugar into a heavy-bottomed saucepan or frying pan. It's best to use a pan that has a pale interior so you can monitor the colour of the caramel easily. Warm the sugar over a medium heat. It will begin to melt – stir it a little with a wooden spoon to encourage it to melt evenly. Lower the heat a bit and leave to melt completely without stirring until the sugar is a rich, dark shade of amber. Quickly tip the caramel over the walnuts on the prepared tray and use a couple of forks to ensure each one is coated. Leave to cool, then chop roughly, leaving some bigger shards for decoration.

In a large bowl, whip the cream until thickened, being careful not to overbeat as it will continue to thicken as it sits. Then use a rubber spatula to fold in the caramel or dulce de leche – just ripple it through, you don't want it to be completely combined.

Drain the raisins from the sherry. Drink the sherry.

Now, thank god, the easy bit: assembly. Use a large bowl – I like to use a big glass trifle bowl so you can see all the beautiful layers. Break up a third of the meringues into large-ish chunks and tip them into the bottom of the bowl. Cover with a layer of cream, then with a handful of raisins and praline. Repeat until all the ingredients are used up, ending with a scattering of praline and raisins and some generous shards of meringue. Cover and chill for at least 6 hours before serving.

TIP

Any leftovers can be put through an ice cream maker just as they are to make a profoundly delicious ice cream.

~

Make your
own menus
~

I APPRECIATE THIS BOOK ISN'T DIVIDED into conventional sections – soups, salads, fish, meat, desserts and so on. I've created some menus here using the recipes in these pages; you may want to follow them, or you may prefer to use them as a springboard for your own ideas. There are no rules really, other than it's good to balance out sharp, sweet, salty, creamy (and also light and stodgy), so each element can shine without being overwhelmed by another.

While I have your attention, I want to share with you something I believe most profoundly: not every component of your meal should be a recipe. We have all been subjected to those plates that feel terribly overwrought, where the fish is fighting for attention, as the vegetables compete in the how-much-seasoning Olympics. It is so soothing to be presented with a superlatively seasoned and cooked dish, which needs nothing more than some gently buttered rice, roast potatoes, steamed beans or a green salad. Hold your nerve. The other principle I hold dear is that there is no shame in buying in. Serve some great charcuterie, olives and crisps in place of a cooked starter. Buy a tart or some great ice cream instead of making a pudding. Don't turn cooking for your best belovèds into an endurance test. Enjoy yourself. There is no dish in the world as sweet as that.

Spring lunch

World-beating Bloody Marys,
page 126

Asparagus new potato and
pea frittata, page 111

The roast chicken that goes
with everything, page 56,
with roast carrots and green salad

Halva ice cream with
sesame brittle, page 47, or
any delicious bought ice cream

~

Weekend dinner

Smoked haddock in tarragon cream,
page 25

Roast lamb with Durham salad,
page 17, roast carrots and potatoes

Farmers' market green salad,
page 27

Bought ice cream or a nice tart

~

Summer party in the garden

Sliced salamis, crudités, hummus,
herb dip, crisps

Sticky honey chicken wings,
page 104

Grilled pomegranate quail,
page 44

Grilled onion salad, page 40

Green and black salad,
page 62

Lemony roast cauliflower
with almonds and curd cheese,
page 67

Margarita pie, page 211 – you might
need two, or some bought ice cream,
if you have lots of people

~

Autumn lunch

Beetroot in horseradish sour cream,
page 221, with some smoked salmon

Carbonnade de boeuf, page 139

Rustic pear galette, page 256

Johann's soda bread, page 268,
with cheeses and figs

~

Prepare-ahead dinner

Johann's soda bread, page 268,
with smoked salmon or smoked
trout, butter and lemon

Duck Parmentier, page 60,
with green beans

Plum cake, page 181, with whipped
cream, slightly sweetened with a
little icing sugar and a splash of
vanilla extract

~

Birthday feast

Greyhound cocktails, page 95,
and champagne

Huîtres gratinées, page 241

Steaks, with salsa verde, page 176,
some grilled endive and/or chips

Meringues for Queen Sophia,
page 270

~

Fireside tea

Egg and watercress sandwiches,
page 267

Potato, Cheddar and spring
onion rolls, page 108

Buttermilk lemon scones,
page 79

Burnt honey and walnut cake,
page 186

Ginger, cardamom and lemon
pryaniki, page 232

~

Apéro hour

Crisps

Gruyere and anchovy puffs,
page 128

Olives sétoises, page 238

Marseillanais cocktail, page 238

Champagne

~

Weekend lunch with friends

Anchovy butter with radishes,
page 102

Julia's pimento cheese, page 171

Whole roast sea bass, page 130

Quick berry crostata, page 133,
with vanilla ice cream

~

Rainy day supper

Leek and ham hock steamed pudding,
page 14, with carrots and green beans

Poached quince with rosemary
and honey, page 122, with thick
Greek yoghurt

~

Acknowledgements

~

I owe an enormous debt of gratitude to everyone at Penguin Michael Joseph, particularly to my brilliant editor Ione Walder, who understood from the first moment what I wanted this book to be and allowed me the freedom to hammer it into life. Thank you also to Agatha Russell for keeping us all on track, to Sarah Fraser, Gail Jones and Daniel Prescott-Bennett for making it look so wonderful, and Annie Lee for her keen attention to the words.

At Peters Fraser + Dunlop, I owe so much to Tessa David for pushing me at the beginning of lockdown in 2020 to write the proposal for this book, and for pushing me generally, in the most enthusiastic, irrepressible and delightful way. She is a force of nature. And also to Laurie Robertson, who steered me through the latter parts of writing this book with her characteristic gentle good humour and thoughtfulness.

Everyone should have a Julia Leonard in their lives. If you don't have one, I advise you to find one as soon as possible. Julia is my dear friend, sounding board, first reader and relentless recipe tester. Her meticulousness is matched only by her enormous kindness and unfailing good humour. I don't know where I would be without you, Julia, but it certainly wouldn't be here.

Thank you also to Zach and Lila Leonard for their relentless and selfless recipe testing.

To the peerless Laura Edwards. I pinched myself when you agreed to take the photographs for this book, and every second was a delight. Thank you, too, to Jo Cowan and Matthew Hague, for assisting, coffee, yoga stretches, and keeping us all going. Joss Herd, food stylist of dreams, for all of the wonderful cooking, irrepressible cheerfulness and wisdom, and El Kemp (I am sorry we didn't get to be neighbours for longer). To my darling Tabitha Hawkins, who bears her gifts so lightly and yet there is no safer pair of prop-styling hands. Mad love to you all for understanding what I wanted this book to be and bringing it to life in a way that was even more beautiful – and so much more fun – than I ever could have imagined. Let's do it again.

Endless thanks to my original cast, Victoria Harper, Helder Daude, Richard Arnold, Stuart Carter, Shona and Louise Clelland, Alex Sanz, Howard Wilmot, Tim Roney, Julian Linley, Kim Fitzsimmons, Steve Larthe de Langeladure, Victoria and Peter White, Vanessa Miner, Damian Grogan and Brian Chapman – angels at my table always. And also to my Stoke Newington family, Liz Vater, Pete Brown, Kate Weston, Nick Perry, Andrew Grace, Nash Khandekar, Lola Borg, and Jo Adams from Stoke Newington Book Shop.

My online friends who became real-life friends, Thane Prince, Melanie Jappy, Romy Gill, Signe Johansen, Catherine Phipps, Charlotte Mendleson, Audrey Gillan, Diana Henry, Lisa Markwell, Sue Quinn, Nicola Miller and Rachel McCormack. Thank you for always providing the highest-quality displacement activity with the least possible prompting.

And my Tas Firin gang, Fiona Kirkpatrick, Lucy Inglis and Lucy Fisher; I hope we can feast on lamb chops and Blossom Hill before too long. How surprisingly delicious.

My brilliant editor at *Delicious.* magazine, Karen 'Bordeaux' Barnes, for her endless patience, support and encouragement, and my editors on the 'Notes from a Small Kitchen Island' column at *The Daily Telegraph*, Tory Young, Simon Lewis and Paul Davies, for indulging my passions, foreign and domestic.

To Nigella Lawson, who tweeted that I should write a book, so I wrote a book. And Mark Diacono, who nagged me and offered excellent counsel, except when it came to football.

My parents, Bryan and Wendy Robertson, and my brother, Grahame Robertson, for eating everything with enthusiasm, or at least without complaint.

And finally, my husband, Séan, for absolutely everything, always. I love you.

Index

~

a

afternoon tea 120–21

aïoli 240–41

   olives Sétoises 238–40

Aleppo pepper *see* pul biber

almonds: how to toast 258–9

   granola for health 125

   lemony roast cauliflower, with almonds and curd cheese 67–8

anchovies: anchovy butter and radishes 102–3

   Gruyère and anchovy puffs 128–9

   salsa verde 176

apples: chicken and apple shoes for Gracie 159

   tarte Tatin 201–3

   Vanessa's De Beauvoir chutney 166–7

asparagus, new potatoes and peas frittata 111

b

bacon, red pepper and feta frittata 112

barley: golubtsy 223–6

basil: salsa verde 176

beans: green and black salad 62–3

beef: Auntie Louie's corned beef and potato pie 11–13

   carbonnade de boeuf 139–41

   chicken-fried steak 208–210

   macaronade Sétoise 252–4

   Stokey Lit Fest chilli 30–33

beer: carbonnade de boeuf 139–41

beetroot: how to roast 221–3

   beetroot in horseradish sour cream 221

biber salçasi: lamb and chickpea soup with minted yoghurt 41–3

biscuits: ginger, cardamom and lemon pryaniki 232–3

   see also cookies

blackberries: quick berry crostata 133–5

blackcurrants: quick berry crostata 133–5

blood oranges: blood orange seed cake 191–2

   Negroni marmalade 167–9

   rhubarb, rosewater and vanilla jam 76

Bloody Mary 126

blueberries: quick berry crostata 133–5

bread: eggs Benedict strata 88–90

   Johann's soda bread 268–9

   see also sandwiches; toast

brioche: Roquefort, figs and honey on brioche 154

brown food 137–8

brunch 85–7

burnt honey and walnut cake 186–8

butter: anchovy butter and radishes 102–3

buttermilk 80, 269

   buttermilk lemon scones 79–80

   Johann's soda bread 268

c

cabbage: golubtsy 223–6

cakes 179–80

   blood orange seed cake 191–2

   burnt honey and walnut cake 186–8

   chocolate and prune cake 189–91

   plum cake 181–2

huîtres gratinées 241–3
  smoked mackerel and spinach with
    horseradish cream frittata 113
spring onions: potato, Cheddar and spring
  onion rolls 108
steak: chicken-fried steak 208–210
steamed pudding: leek and ham hock steamed
  pudding 14–16
stews 137–8
Stoke Newington 21–4, 27, 30
strata: eggs Benedict strata 88–90
swede: Vanessa's De Beauvoir chutney 166–7

t

tarragon: Fox Reformed smoked haddock in
  tarragon cream 25–7
  garlicky tarragon mushrooms on
    toast 152–3
tarte Tatin 201–3
tequila: Meemaw's margarita pie 211–12
Texas 205–6
tielle Sétoise 244–6
toast 147–8
  garlicky tarragon mushrooms on
    toast 152–3
  Roquefort, figs and honey on brioche 154
  upside-down French onion soup 149–50
tomato juice: Bloody Mary 126
tomatoes: moules farcies 248–51
  Stokey Lit Fest chilli 30–33
  tielle Sétoise 244–6
Toulouse sausage rolls 108–9
tuna: anchovy butter and radishes 102–3
Turkish Food Centre 37–8
Turkish-ish grilled onion salad 40–41

v

vanilla: plum cake 181–2
  rhubarb, rosewater and vanilla jam 76
  vanilla sugar 182
vermouth: Negroni marmalade 167–9
  see also Noilly Prat
vinaigrette: potato salad 65–6
vodka: Bloody Mary 126
  greyhound cocktail 95–6

w

walnuts: burnt honey and walnut cake 186–8
  Circassian chicken 229–31
weekends 71–2
  guests 115–21
wine: plum cake 181–2

y

yoghurt: halva honey ice cream with sesame
    brittle 47–9
  lamb and chickpea soup with minted
    yoghurt 41–3

PENGUIN MICHAEL JOSEPH

UK | USA | Canada | Ireland | Australia
India | New Zealand | South Africa

Penguin Michael Joseph is part of the Penguin Random House group of companies
whose addresses can be found at global.penguinrandomhouse.com

Penguin
Random House
UK

First published by Penguin Michael Joseph, 2022

001

Set in Neuzeit Office Std Bold, Sabon and Portrait
Colour reproduction by Altaimage Ltd
Printed in Latvia by Livonia Print

The authorized representative in the EEA is Penguin Random House Ireland,
Morrison Chambers, 32 Nassau Street, Dublin D02 YH68

A CIP catalogue record for this book is available from the British Library

ISBN: 978–0–241–50467–3

www.greenpenguin.co.uk